T0339528

"Dr. Wei masterfully confronts the overlooked crisis of physician burnout with a practical approach for reclaiming wellbeing. This is more than a book, it's a movement that transforms a daunting and complex challenge into actionable steps ensuring the wellbeing of healthcare's most vital resource: its physicians."
– **Kari Granger,** CEO of The Granger Network, Executive Advisory

"This book is long overdue and no one is better qualified to write it than Julie. As an exemplar physician and surgeon, she hits the mark with brilliance."
– **Jim Loehr, EdD,** Renowned Performance Psychologist and Co-Founder of the Human Performance Institute

"Dr. Julie Wei is a champion. Her commitment to the wellbeing of others knows no bounds. This is the ultimate playbook for physicians and those in training to 'win' and achieve incredible wellbeing in their life and careers."
– **Lou Holtz,** Legendary Hall of Fame football coach, motivational speaker, author, TV analyst, and philanthropist

"Dr. Julie Wei is an important and brilliant and compassionate physician voice. We encourage everyone to read this book."
– **Scott Becker,** Becker's Healthcare

"Are you one of the many physicians I know who are annoyed by admonitions from others to become more resilient? Truth be told, the physicians I know are already the most resilient professionals I know! If you are committed to your own well-being (as are most resilient persons), then this book is for you. Checklists used in clinical practice have been systematically developed based on best evidence and consensus. They are familiar tools in clinical practice. Dr. Wei developed this approach to offer physicians standardized and achievable solutions in a set of checklists designed to mitigate physician burnout and increase physician wellbeing. If you are a medical student, resident, or fellow, these checklists will be invaluable as you launch your career as a physician. Dr. Wei shares many of her own experiences that bring to life the need for a more systematic approach for fostering personal, professional, and psychological safety."
– **R. Kevin Grigsby,** Co-author: Grigsby RK, Mallon WT. *Thriving: New Perspectives and Approaches for Personal and Organizational Success.* AAMC Successful Medical School Department Chairs Series. Washington, DC: AAMC, 2020.

"Dr. Wei has provided us with practical and meaningful strategies to approach these important issues. This book itself warrants its own place on a very important checklist!"
– **Jennifer Shin, MD, SM,** Department of Otolaryngology-Head and Neck Surgery, Department of Surgery, Office for Faculty Affairs, Harvard Medical School

"This is a must-read for all physicians in today's environment of production pressure, burnout, and disengagement. Dr. Wei's journey is a familiar one for all of us and her heartfelt advice and her willingness to be vulnerable and share her personal battles is truly touching and valuable."
– **Butch Uejima, MD, MMM, FAAP, CPHRM,** Vice President, Chief Medical Officer & Chair Dept of Pediatric Anesthesiology & Perioperative Medicine, Nemours Children's Health, Delaware Valley

Safeguarding Physician Wellbeing

The United States is facing a worsening epidemic of physician burnout with unprecedented numbers of them leaving the workforce and practice of clinical medicine across all career stages. The prevalence of physician burnout has accelerated through COVID-19, resulting in an anticipated serious national shortage of physicians within the current decade amidst an increased proportion of aging and unhealthy population.

The critical shortage of physicians coupled with an unhealthy physician workforce results in longer wait times for access, continued increased healthcare costs, decreased quality of care, and worsening patient experience.

Despite increasing media coverage, published data, and identification of system-based factors that erode physician wellbeing, no standardized systematic solution has been implemented across hospitals, health systems, or a variety of employment models or practice settings for any or all doctors regardless of whether they are primary care, medical, or surgical subspecialists.

Effective solutions to mitigate physician burnout, protect current working physicians, and keep them from leaving medicine require a *SHIFT* and a more individualized approach. Many proposed academic models address system-based factors, but such solutions depend greatly on those who employ doctors. Executive leadership in charge of healthcare systems are often challenged by physician burnout and their desired autonomy, against the need for standardization of care delivery to improve quality and decrease cost. Physician productivity measures continue to be based on data samples of physician compensation surveys supplied by companies like Sullivan Cotter or Medical Group Management Association (MGMA). Such benchmarks are commonly used but data may not reflect specific realities for any organizations nor the rapid changes in the landscape of US healthcare amidst mergers, acquisitions, consolidation, and shifts in employment models from insurance and online retail giants and private equity.

This book uses a "checklist" approach to empower any medical student, resident, fellow, or practicing physician to create and experience psychological, personal, and professional safety and wellbeing. Not only can individual physicians choose and use these checklists themselves, but those who live with, love, and cherish one or more physicians in their families and/or lives can use this book to understand physician realities and their risks.

Safeguarding Physician Wellbeing

Using Checklists for Personal, Professional, and Psychological Safety

Julie L. Wei, MD, MMM, FAAP

Routledge
Taylor & Francis Group

A PRODUCTIVITY PRESS BOOK

First published 2024
by Routledge
605 Third Avenue, New York, NY 10158

and by Routledge
4 Park Square, Milton Park, Abingdon, Oxon, OX14 4RN

Routledge is an imprint of the Taylor & Francis Group, an informa business

ISBN: 978-1-032-58990-9 (hbk)
ISBN: 978-1-032-58989-3 (pbk)
ISBN: 978-1-003-45247-8 (ebk)

DOI: 10.4324/9781003452478

Typeset in Adobe Garamond Pro
by SPi Technologies India Pvt Ltd (Straive)

To Dave

You sacrificed personally and professionally beyond measure, while I struggled and didn't know how to help myself. I am here today because you have been my harbor, shelter, pillar of strength, and light, during utter darkness. Our family and Claire fueled my ability to care for and give to others. May I always be a source of love, joy, laughter, and safety for you.

To Claire

Your smiles, voice, laughter, sarcasm, and jokes always made me feel better no matter how long or hard my days were caring for others. Your hugs are like oxygen. You made me a better doctor, surgeon, and adult, from the moment you came into the world. Thank you for the gift of motherhood. May I show you with my life and actions, the joy of serving and helping others. I wish you a chance to be a doctor if you choose, and to have great doctors who are WELL when you need them.

To My Parents

Thank you for your sacrifices, hard work, financial support, and love. Because of you, I was able to achieve the best educational journey and have the most incredible life so far. You taught me work ethic like no other and taught yourselves how to navigate the complex US Health System and stayed as healthy as possible. You showed me how to be resourceful and resilient, from the day we arrived in this country. You broadened my perspective on what matters the most to patients.

To Nancy

You are the best sister and best friend, constant companion, and my emotional support human since you were born. Despite our 11-year age difference, I have been blessed because you have provided psychological safety for me throughout my life. You listen with empathy and compassion, your intellect challenged my perspectives, and you validate my emotions. Thank you for supporting me through all my life events, best and worst.

To Herdley

Thank you for your incredible career focused entirely on supporting physicians and their wellbeing. You are always the light and safe shelter during the darkness, for me and countless physicians, surgeons, and trainees. By giving permission and teaching physicians how to process pain and suffering, you show each to be a light that can shine brightly again. Thank you for validating the pain and suffering physicians endure and healing them so they may heal others. Your impact to physicians and their loved ones/families is immeasurable. I am forever grateful for our shared journey, where every starfish that is out of the safe ocean, are picked up with compassion, love, then returned to safety.

Contents

Author Bio

Julie L. Wei, MD, MMM, FAAP, is a Pediatric Otolaryngologist and new Division Director, the Dr. Alfred J. Magoline Chair of Otolaryngology, at Akron Children's Hospital in Akron Ohio. She is also a Professor of Otolaryngology Head Neck Surgery at University of Cincinnati College of Medicine and faculty in the ENT Division at Cincinnati Children's Hospital Medical Center.

Dr. Wei obtained her medical degree from New York Medical College, followed by ENT residency training at Mayo Clinic Rochester. She completed 2 years of fellowship training at the now Lurie Children's Hospital in Chicago. In May 2023, she completed a master's in medical management from Carnegie Mellon University's Heinz College of Information Systems and Public Policy. Dr. Wei has served in many leadership roles including Surgeon-in-Chief, Director, GME Wellbeing Initiative, Chair of Medical Staff Health and Wellness Committee at Nemours Children's Hospital Orlando, and as Chair of Otolaryngology Education and Advisor for Association of Women Surgeons at University of Central Florida College of Medicine for the past near decade. She is the immediate past president of American Society of Pediatric Otolaryngology and past president of Society of Ear, Nose, Throat Advances for Children.

In 2019, Dr. Wei developed intermittent right shoulder pain for which she underwent injections. By April of 2021 during pandemic onset, she developed a frozen shoulder in middle of endoscopic surgery. This resulted in a decompression surgery after which she never thought she would struggle with losing nearly all range of motion despite physical therapy. Six months later, cervical radiculopathy symptoms on the same side developed from 4-level degenerative discs with compression of C5-C6. Severe shoulder and neck pain and constant paresthesia of the right hand resulted in an unfathomable decision to take first short-, then long-term medical leave. In February 2022, she made the difficult decision to take a *"PAUSE"* in clinical and surgical practice to pursue total healing without surgical intervention, while living with uncertainty about her career in surgery.

During her time away from practice, Dr. Wei devoted unprecedented time to her body, undergoing scheduled chiropractic care, cervical and lumbar decompression therapy, physiotherapy/massages, and routine work out with strength training to reverse the completely atrophic right rotator cuff muscles due to frozen shoulder. Grieving and processing the trauma associated with her disability also fueled her passion to increase awareness in surgeons on surgical ergonomics, WRMSD, and permission to seek help through writing and speaking on her journey from injury to recovery. At the ASPO annual meeting in May 2023, Dr. Wei moderated a panel on surgical ergonomics to highlight prevalence in her subspecialty, risk factors, and preventive measures. Dr. Wei has spent 2 decades helping children and families avoid unnecessary medications and surgical procedures through nutrition and health literacy and eliminating ENT symptoms through healthier dietary habits. She has also been a champion of supporting mental health for surgeons, by addressing the stigma and lack of support for surgeons who invariably experience PTSD.

Dr. Wei has authored two books on how dietary habits in children can cause acid reflux, ENT symptoms, and subsequent misdiagnosis and over treatment with use of medications. She is a TEDx speaker and her talk, "The Hidden Dangers of the Milk and Cookie Disease" has been viewed over 408,000 times since 2015. Dr. Wei has created online courses on her website on treating ENT symptoms through dietary modification. She has published over 49 peer-reviewed articles, 13 invited articles, and 12 book chapters.

Foreword

I first met Julie when she was a student in the Master of Medical Management program at Carnegie Mellon University. I previously had been a student there and credit the program to opening my eyes to possibilities I had never considered. Because of the tremendous impact the program had on my own career, I have been teaching there ever since. Julie and I had many conversations about the impact of burnout on physicians and her assignments were always incredibly insightful. Several years have passed since then and the importance of physician wellness couldn't be more important to physicians and society in general. I was excited to review this book because of the critical nature of addressing physician well-being and its use of the checklist approach. As a pediatric critical care doctor for almost 30 years, I remember the introduction of checklists into standard use and the reluctance many of us had in using them. As Julie mentions, to-do lists were used by all the pediatric residents I trained with, and we felt like we never got to the end of the list. The use of checklists is quite different as they are specific to a task and ensure accurate and timely completion of that task. They are now in routine use throughout healthcare and have been written about including the well-known *The Checklist Manifesto* by Atul Gawande.

Before reading this book, I wouldn't have thought of using checklists to help with physician well-being, much less writing a book on the topic. As I read the first few chapters, I got more excited about the approach. I am an avid reader and run a monthly book club at my own organization (Cincinnati Children's). At the end of many of the books, some will comment "that was interesting, but there were very few actionable steps to take that the book provided." That couldn't be further from the truth with this book. Each chapter has actionable, easy-to-use checklists that are specific, action-oriented, and can easily be finished. Some are general and applicable to many professionals and others are more specifically oriented to physicians. As I read the chapter on financial checklists, it was like a highlight reel of many of the financial mistakes I made coming out of training. It is even more critical that physicians entering residency training take steps to protect their financial well-being. According to the Medscape Physician Wealth and Debt report in 2023, the average graduating medical student has a combined debt of 251,000 dollars. Most then train for a minimum of three years at lower wages and many train at least twice that long. Every medical student in the United States would likely benefit from the succinct financial advice provided within.

One other area worth addressing is the approach of having a specific physician wellness program. Burnout is ever in the healthcare setting, was exacerbated by the pandemic, and is an issue for almost all who work in this environment. Many organizations now have employee wellness programs that target all employees with varying degrees of success. Others have specific physician programs, and now some are providing unique programs for physicians with a different program for others. Certainly, any effort to improve the well-being of those working in the complex and ever-changing healthcare environment is worthy. I believe this book makes a good case for the importance of an approach that is tied to the unique pressures facing physicians today. The checklist approach will feel familiar to today's physicians, be actionable, and can be used as a reference at different times both as a whole and individual chapters.

Steve Davis MD, MMM, MS
President and CEO, Cincinnati Children's Hospital Medical Center

Preface

In 2007, the World Health Organization (WHO) launched the "Safe Surgery Save Lives" slogan with a declared goal to reduce deaths related to surgical procedures around the world. In 2008, they piloted the use of a "Safe Surgery Checklist" in eight hospitals around the world, to reduce complications related to surgeries such as surgical site infections. This was a transformational initiative with a clear and concrete action-based initiative that required shared awareness and enhanced communication without requiring significant resources by members in any operating room. By January 2009, the National Health Service in the UK mandated the standardized use of this checklist.

By 2011, thought leader, surgeon, and author Dr. Atul Gawande published *The Checklist Manifesto: How to Get Things Right*. In this book, Dr. Gawande shared the risk and commonality of errors of ineptitude (mistakes made because people don't make propose use of what they know) prevalent in healthcare settings. Even the most competent surgeon can make mistakes while performing routine tasks, due to the increasing volume and complexity of knowledge, especially in healthcare delivery. The book includes data which show that professionals in any industry are at risk of making mistakes when performing under high stress and in pressured environments. The most poignant message is that by using something as simple as a checklist, many professions beyond medicine and disaster recovery, can create improvements in how we achieve desired outcomes through daily work.

My Journey as a Physician

I finished my surgical training from 1996 to 2001 at the Mayo Clinic Rochester, to become an ear, nose, and throat physician and surgeon. I then spent two years in fellowship training so that I would become a pediatric ENT, an ear, nose, and throat doctor and surgeon who only treats children from birth to age 18 (now extended to 21 or even older in many pediatric health systems). For the first decade of my career, I worked as a faculty at an academic medical center as a part of the Department of Otolaryngology-Head Neck Surgery because I loved teaching and wanted to help train residents and fellows. Due to being a pediatric subspecialist, I worked both at the tertiary free-standing children's hospital in Kansas City, as well as at the university satellite clinic and ambulatory surgery center. Back then, surgeons were not required to lead, nor perform, any pre-procedure "timeout" using a checklist with the Operating Room (OR) team.

Fast forward to 2013. I made the difficult decision to leave Kansas City, move to Orlando, and started my new leadership role as a Division Chief, at a new children's hospital, part of a large pediatric health system, still seeing patients in clinic and performing surgeries. This was when I learned about, then became a champion, for using this standardized process to ensure optimal patient safety. Not only did I personally use the WHO surgery checklist before every case, but during my role as Surgeon-in-Chief from 2016 to 2019 for the hospital, I emphasized compliance by every surgeon, proceduralist, and the entire OR team, in following this process to minimize risks to patients who underwent anesthesia and surgeries.

Given my role and responsibility to review and address preventable harm and system-based errors that could have, or did, cause patient harm, I learned in depth the consequences of both lack of solid policies and processes as well as when they are not followed consistently by humans. I had the privilege of meeting and hearing John Nance, author of *Why Hospitals Should Fly: The Ultimate Flight Plan to Patient Safety and Quality Care*. Mr. Nance shared the use of "checklists" and principles developed and adopted by the aviation industry, after the deadliest accident in aviation history at Tenerife airport on March 27, 1977, with 583 fatalities from the collision of two 747 passenger jets. Yet, 583 fatalities pale in comparison to the estimated 250,000 or more patient deaths annually, as medical error is the third leading cause of death in the US after heart disease and cancer. Every time I get on a commercial flight for travel, I am relieved and grateful that checklist(s) are uniformly used to ensure my safety and that of all fellow passengers and crew members.

This book was written, inspired by over a decade of efforts addressing my own burnout and that of countless colleagues. My "a-ha" moment was the realization that we can help every practicing doctor, including those in training, understand WHY and HOW they too can use checklists for their own safety. Checklists can help physicians take actions that increase their own safety and wellbeing, regardless of what type of doctor they are, primary care or specialist, where they work, and does not depend on whether their employer provides resources for physician wellbeing. Just as patient safety is optimized for surgery through the use of a checklist surgeons follow for all pre-incision "timeout", checklists that address the unique risks faced by physicians can be used to address the worsening epidemic of physician burnout but using a completely novel approach.

The checklists outlined in each chapter are designed to create personal, professional, and psychological safety for any trainee and physician so that their individual and collective wellbeing will increase regardless of gender, specialties or primary care, employer models, geography, and practice settings. It's time to *SHIFT* away from the implied or explicit expectation that doctors are responsible for "fixing" their own burnout by simply doing yoga, meditation, and "self-care". While activities that may define "self-care" and personal accountability are important and relevant, what America desperately needs is a clear understanding by both the physicians themselves, as well as the public and those who employ physicians, the realities of our broken "system", unhealthy attitudes, and culture, in how physicians are trained not to acknowledge their fundamental needs as a human being, same as all the patients they care for.

The impact of the pandemic exacerbated erosions of mental health for physicians, already burnt "crips" in an increasingly pressured culture of margin and productivity over their core values of service and building trust in the sacred relationships enjoyed between physicians and patients. Between professional moral distress and physician's own human needs and life demands, this has contributed to a rapidly shrinking US physician workforce over the past several years. Whether a physician chooses partial, or total, adoption of each suggestion on any checklist in this book, each has been created ONLY with the physician in mind, aimed to protect any physicians over the course of their careers in clinical practice. Physicians are not the only ones who are "burned out", the use of the checklists outlined in this book can be modified to address burnout in nursing and other roles in healthcare, as well as for other professions.

I was taught by an incredible counselor, Dr. Herdley Paolini, who has worked with physicians for over 30 years, that despite the reality of inescapable suffering as a physician, I can learn to "*suffer WELL*". Having endured much unanticipated suffering personally, professionally, and psychologically, all the while experiencing the immense gifts from a career as a teacher, healer, surgeon, mentor, colleague, and self-grown "protector" of fellow physicians, I created these "checklists" to help other physicians "suffer well" and increase career longevity instead of leaving the practice of medicine.

When a physician suffers, the ripple effect and negative impact on their families, loved ones, and community are nearly never addressed. To live one's life and career in "scarcity" of time and life, feeling "robbed" of being fully available to self and loved ones, is a tragedy and perhaps unnecessary. Losing autonomy in countless aspects of how physicians perform their daily work, erosion of the physician identity and "worth" to one measured by their "productivity", have created poor value alignment between physicians and their employers. This is a source of constant moral distress and can create in physicians, unrelenting internal conflict that has accelerated the widespread "burnout" in our profession.

Years of giving my "all", in every aspect of my performance, was to prove that as a woman, an Asian immigrant, and a female surgeon, I was and am "good" enough, "better than", and "deserve" to be "*here*" (at all points in time during my training and career). Just like thousands of other physicians, I too experienced feeling underappreciated and undervalued, and lived an exhaustive daily experience of my life like a hamster running on a wheel that simply spun faster without the ability to stop or get off. The courage to take first a short, then long-term, leave of absence, was only made possible because I had developed unanticipated injury, progressive pain, and eventual admission of medical disability in my right shoulder and neck and losing range of motion of my right shoulder despite decompression surgery.

How fascinating that by taking the unthinkable "time out", a break from over 20 years of overscheduled years of busy practice, I was able to experience healing of both my mind and body. This period of personal and professional "*renewal*" has been the ultimate gift I would *never* have given myself. The struggle to navigate disability, the decision to take a break, fighting for disability benefits, exploring employment options and limitations due to a noncompete agreement I signed 10 years ago without any clue that it would impact my ability to provide for my family. The accumulation of both professional and personal trauma, from being sued to having PTSD-like symptoms from severe patient bleeding out after tonsillectomy, infertility struggles, and losing my professional identity and income, have all taught me *HOW* to embrace uncertainty, anxiety, fear, and the unknown. I found new strength from within despite not having my "identity" as an employed physician, surgeon, and someone of "worth" by the current US Healthcare System and societal measures.

I was so lucky to have made the decision to return to school during the onset of the pandemic and completed my Masters in Medical Management at Carnegie Mellon University Heinz School of Information Systems and Policy, from 2021 to 2023. The experience provided increased depth and broadened my knowledge of the challenges I faced daily in practice. It was a privilege to feel a sense of "belonging", to a group of highly intellectual and talented physicians who all wanted to create positive change in the US healthcare delivery and grow their own leadership journey. Going back to school made me highly energized while giving me a new sense of purpose. During my time away from practice, I often woke in the middle of the night feeling a sense of panic, missing my professional identity, beloved patients, and colleagues who were all I had ever known. Anxiety about income for our family, as well as my health and uncertain future at age 52, was hard to explain to any physicians unless they too had experienced such.

Finally, during my year of serving as President of our national pediatric ENT society, much reading, connecting with countless professionals outlined in this book, fearlessly applying to jobs that I never heard back from, and accepting many rejections, all inspired this book. I am beyond grateful to have regained my health and professional identity again as a pediatric ENT surgeon, and the ability to support my own family. I have returned to clinical care, with the opportunity to work collaboratively with two incredible children's hospitals and health systems, amongst incredible colleagues and care teams. My heart is once again so full as I have the privilege and opportunity to care for children and their families. May the readers, current and future physicians, feel and be safe should they ever face unexpected challenges personally, professionally, and psychologically. Perhaps these checklists will help physicians move from surviving to thriving, live with self-compassion, and most importantly take control and create autonomy in how we address physician burnout by creating our own safety.

Introduction

Why Checklists? How Checklists Can Help Physicians Achieve Safety and Wellbeing

Checklists are commonly used in daily life for personal or professional use and can range from simple lists like a "to-do" list, errands, or grocery lists, to more complicated checklists that are mandatory to ensure absolute safety for operating complex machinery like aviation protocols followed by pilots.

I have several "to-do" lists, on my phone, laptop, and even Post It notes, just to make sure I don't forget anything. The years of cramming every thought, and self-imposed tasks that feel like they will make or break our lives at home and at work, have led to unhealthy anxiety due to the feeling of never completing all tasks on my "lists".

In contrast, checklists are critical in healthcare settings because they are not subjective nor individually created. Instead, for example, the pre-incision World Health Organization timeout checklist, and the handoff checklists used between surgeons, anesthesiologists, and doctors in charge of the patient in intensive care units (ICU) or nurses, and doctor-to-doctor handoffs across all units during daily shift changes, between services, from one area of the hospital to another, are all systematically developed based on best evidence and consensus. Safe outcomes are only possible because of the repetition of using the same and reliable checklists that ensure the most critical of information and actions have been taken to protect the patient.

The sense of urgency for this book and the idea to promote a checklist-based approach to address physician burnout and increase physician wellbeing is based on the massive need to address the current lack of standardized and achievable solutions to protect any physician and those training to become one. The immense pressures for doctors to be perfect are based on societal and self-imposed expectations and the desire to protect each and every patient in an increasingly

DOI: 10.4324/9781003452478-1

1

complex and highly stressful work environment in delivering healthcare in any setting. The unrelenting pressure for physicians to "produce" and generate profit margins against the ever-rising cost of US healthcare delivery in every setting, has continued to increase based on increased budgets set by employers of physicians.

Doctors are measured and assessed in many ways as factory workers in assembly lines except without the exact repetitive, predictable, and simplistic tasks. Instead, amidst highly variable population of patients, medical issues, language barriers, social determinants of health, mental health, and other issues that any physician can't "treat" and correct during a medical visit, doctors are measured by the total number of patients they see each half or full day, how quickly they see them, and each patient visit translates into relative value units or "*RVUs*". Essentially, interactions with patients in the outpatient world are measures of "business transactions" in the healthcare industry.

For doctors who work primarily in shifts caring for hospitalized patients such as hospitalists who care for those outside ICUs and intensivists (doctors who oversee care for very ill and complex patients in the ICU), their work demands are influenced by how many patients they are responsible for during each shift. Rounding (seeing and assessing patients), reviewing test results, constant decision making for very ill patients, coordinating care with specialists consulted, and planning discharge becomes challenged depending on doctor to patients ratio and other factors impacting each member on the care team. Additionally, language barriers, social issues faced by the patient including food and housing insecurity, lack of resources once discharged, and the enormous mental stress endured by physicians who are expected and want to address all such issues for every patient, can overwhelm the most competent of physicians.

It is beyond the scope of this book to dive into the many factors which influence how doctors are perceived, valued, treated, and measured in our healthcare system today, complicated by insurance companies and our healthcare payment systems with various reimbursement rates, Centers for Medicare & Medicaid Services (CMS) and government regulations, health policy and health law. The most critically important but often not discussed factor that directly impacts both patients and physicians today, is how politics and politicians have inserted their ideology and agenda to influence care and consequences on public health without necessarily regard for facts, data, and science.

Despite a worsening shortage of healthcare workers including nurses, physicians, various technicians, and medical staff who work in all clinics, hospitals and health systems seem to be building more facilities to expand their footprint and geographic reach, and compete for patients as *"market shares"* against other health systems. There is no shortage of satellite clinics, urgent cares, emergency rooms, or new hospitals, along with mergers and acquisitions and now private equity owning and running primary care and specialty practices. Hence, the demand for hiring those who provide the actual frontline care continues to rise, especially after three years since pandemic onset. Additional factors that influence physician burnout include the failure of various intended policies to decrease the cost of healthcare while providing better patient outcomes and experiences.

New awareness and emphasis on the need for more efficient and equitable access for patients include competition by retail giants, insurance companies, and various-sized private equity investment companies, to employ doctors and advanced practitioners. All such potential employers have multiple ways to entice the public in how they interact and use services with convenience and access being the key drivers for success. The pandemic didn't create physician burnout but certainly accelerated at least a decade-long worsening of wellbeing for doctors and healthcare workers. Mass gun violence across the nation, including those enacted in healthcare settings, doctor's offices, and by patients with mental health issues, has created unprecedented and indescribable degrees and depth of stress for physicians today.

Checklists have not been leveraged, in a holistic approach, to create personal, professional, and psychological safety for physicians. Doing so will increase their wellbeing and massively increase their psychological safety. Instead, employer-specific wellness programs are often not specific to physicians, nor are countless programs and emphasis on "resilience" as if physicians aren't resilient enough. All such programs may have some benefit but are variable, inadequate, and noncomprehensive to ensure as many physicians are supported to protect those at risk.

Each of the following chapters will address a topic of importance that puts physicians at risks, and provide suggested actions through checklists that every physician can use to achieve protection throughout their careers against risks of disability, litigation, financial problems, debt management, PTSD, mental health crises, and more to enjoy career longevity. Physicians are not systematically taught of the risks they face in the practice of medicine and surgery, nor how to create a safety net to address what they will endure by choosing this noble profession, until now.

As each physician's needs, personal and professional circumstances, and life and career stages are unique, and as the challenges they face are highly variable at any given time, readers can use and apply checklists as applicable or desired.

CHECKLIST 1 WHY CHECKLISTS HELP PHYSICIANS AND PHYSICIANS IN TRAINING

■ Every medical student, resident, fellow, and physician can use checklists to make sure they know what actions to take, to create protection against personal and professional risks related to being a physician and being a human.

- Physicians in training as well as when they enter the workforce, will always lack "time" to focus on their own needs. Using checklists will maximize their safety with minimal time requirements.
- Even if doctors are willing to make time to focus on their own needs, most are not taught nor know the right professional, nor right actions to take, to avoid risks and adverse outcomes for their own lives and careers. Checklists will at least get them focused on actions they can and should consider and why.
- Doctors are compulsive about patient care and all decisions they make as well as following up on test results and pretty much all details related to patients, but not themselves. Checklists focused on physician wellbeing allow their families to help them take actions necessary to protect not only the doctor but their loved ones as well.
- Many doctors feel guilty for even thinking about themselves, taking time during normal business hours to go get their annual check-ups, dentist, and countless appointments that seem routine for others. Checklists can remove inner narratives and judgment about being "selfish" and instead help doctors treat various aspects of wellbeing as they do for patients.
- Not every physician is knowledgeable about physician wellbeing nor actions critical to creating personal and professional protection since there is no standardized training on these topics. Checklists will help medical student and trainees so that they are not dependent on "luck" or random chance of having physician teachers who help them take critical action early enough in their careers. Many medical students don't have mentors in the specialties they want to pursue for a career nor those with expertise based on real life and in-depth career experiences.
- Instead of having loved ones and families feeling helpless when watching a physician or physician in training suffer, now those who support the physician in their family and life can understand the risks and actions possible to protect them against unavoidable occupational hazards. Checklists set the foundation for conversations and action plans to mitigate risks facing physicians.
- Checklists always provide a sense of accomplishment, particularly for an entire profession of humans who have been highly competitive, groomed to be even more so just to get into medical school and enter a profession that is highly selective. Help a physician feel better today by encouraging them to use checklists.

Chapter 1

My Journey

I was unaware and ignored the early and all signs of my increasing levels of burnout in the early years of my career. After enduring and completing five years of residency training to become an ear, nose, and throat surgeon, I spent another two years in fellowship training to become a pediatric otolaryngologist so my career would be devoted to caring for children and their families. At the ripe old age of 33, I started my professional job as a surgeon in a new city working as an academic faculty with a department of otolaryngology at a university medical center. During my first year in practice, I also got married and became a first-time house owner. With my long-awaited income, I started paying off my medical school loans which took the next 10 years to pay off.

No training ever taught us the ideal or right "pace" to become a good surgeon, doctor, and academic faculty who also teaches medical students and ENT residents, and how to conduct clinical research while seeing as many patients as possible and gaining experience in surgery. It was frankly exhausting just to get to this point, proving that I deserved the training spot to become a subspecialty surgeon despite being a minority and especially being a woman. To say that the next or first six years of my "career" were "busy" would be an incredible understatement. All I wanted was to do what I thought was expected of me, not only to be a "great" doctor by reputation from referring pediatricians and parents in my community but also to be a highly "productive" surgeon in how much volume of cases I was able to complete in any given operating room day and safely too.

I continued clinical research in topics I came up with, and mentored residents and fellows to complete research so that ours would be accepted for presentation at national meetings and published in scientific journals after rigorous review processes. In addition, doctors in academic jobs are expected and encouraged

DOI: 10.4324/9781003452478-2

to join various national professional societies of their field and serve on various committees at their hospital, organization, and in their societies. After all, one could not be promoted from assistant professor level to associate, then finally to "professor" level, the "holy grail" of academic medicine, without fulfilling long lists of criteria mandated by any academic institution.

While my resume or "curriculum vitae" (cv) and other metrics that measured my success (billing and collection, RVUs, number of publications, etc.) indicated I was a "good" faculty, what was never measured was my ovarian reserve, physical and mental exhaustion, and inability to enjoy any time when away from doing anything that's not related to work. I was and still am not alone.

I achieved a miracle pregnancy and gave birth at almost 36 years of age and struggled with both primary and secondary infertility. I didn't really want to be in the "high risk" category according to OB/GYN doctors due to maternal age. Not meeting my husband Dave until age 32 and marrying at almost 34 was not my plan. As a medical student and then a surgical resident among mostly male residents, female trainees and surgeons are fully immersed in the unspoken stigma associated with pregnancy and having children during their training.

Some female residents are brave enough and have done so, paving the way for others. For most, the idea of dealing with interruption to demanding training, and taking weeks of maternity leave, which would decrease surgical training experience and cases we have to "log", resulting also in our peers in training having to take more calls in our absence, and even the potential of delaying graduation was overwhelming and unthinkable. While male surgical residents and fellows have partners and spouses that bear the pregnancy, and even with current-day paternity leave policies in place for male students and trainees, women physicians face greater challenges including now published data on increased complications related to pregnancy, pregnancy loss, and non-elective C sections.[1]

Fast forward to early promotion in 2009 right before my 40th birthday, I started struggling just to get out of bed by 6 am as I have since 1997 when I started residency. I didn't have visible "injury", yet I had total body aches every morning. Of course, I got up and went to work every day anyway. But somehow realized I was irritable, reactive, and angry most of the time, especially whenever my pager went off or asked to do something else (which occurred several times daily and constantly). Every day, I anxiously dreaded being "late" against my "schedule", regardless of when I was in the clinic or the operating room, nor how "fast" I worked.

Despite doing what I loved, caring for children and their families, and working with great colleagues, there was not much joy. Instead, I felt I was drowning in hopelessness despite making a good salary, being married, achieving the dream of becoming a mother, and then rushing home to cook and be a wife and mother. There was no "break" when rushing from the operating room to drive to the satellite clinics hospital had expanded to whether 15 or 20 miles away. I was late or at risk of being "late" for the next meeting, deadline, project, email reply, inbox response and squeezing another surgery sooner than later for whatever reason. For countless physicians, it takes our every waking second of over-functioning and anticipating, not to "fail" and to achieve near perfection in all that we do. Thousands of faceless physicians have experienced a high degree of "burnout syndrome", defined by Dr. Christina Maslach as *emotional exhaustion, depersonalization, and a reduced sense of personal accomplishment.*

As a first-generation immigrant, Asian female who trained to become an ENT surgeon over 20 years ago, I am writing this book as the ultimate self-guide to warn, protect, and help all physicians based on the suffering and trauma I have endured personally, psychologically, and professionally. While I am grateful to have enjoyed the many aspects of my career, I now wonder if I could been trained to better prepare for the accumulated countless scars from micro- and macroaggression, implicit and explicit bias from patients and others at the workplace, and endured some devastating experiences related to adverse events in my patients for which I didn't know how or from whom to get help when I needed it the most.

The immense negative impact on the mental health of physicians is cumulative over time based on a highly unhealthy culture that teaches students, residents, and young doctors to believe, accept, and self-impose suffering as an absolute. The past decades of healthcare in America have shifted to now nearly ubiquitous "business" culture of "transactions", even if a patient and physician enjoyed a great interaction during their encounter. Pressures to see more and more patients in a single hour, half, or full day in the clinic means those encounters become shorter and shorter, leading to patient complaints and poor ratings. Every day, even nights and weekends, physicians must complete after actual clinics and surgeries, that do not necessarily add quality or value. Physicians lose control in deciding how, when, how many patients they should see, as well as having to answer every "inbox message", patient call, and decreasing boundaries and ability to focus, not having enough staff support, endless phone calls to get prior authorization to order necessary tests, and reduced reimbursement, all of this results in *"moral distress"* from value misalignment that has pushed thousands of physicians to leave their once beloved profession.

Physical, emotional, and mental exhaustion, moral distress, witnessing human tragedies, trauma, PTSD, unanticipated harassment, and now increasing violence and threats from patients, are key reasons why no one should be surprised physicians are leaving the workforce, retiring early, and everyone should be concerned for the wellbeing and safety of physicians.

In recent years after working with hundreds of physician colleagues, I observed them trying to create solutions that create psychological safety and immediate access to mental health counseling specifically for doctors. For some, it's "death" by a thousand cuts, as it's difficult to know what single event, personally and/or professionally, can trigger or cause severe distress for a physician. I learned from my own experience and that of others what physicians really need when they need "help", even when they don't admit it. I have had the opportunity to help facilitate a culture change and create the kind of "help" extremely busy doctors can access anytime they become so distraught such that they can heal and recover. Having experienced unanticipated devastating events I was unprepared for, now I know and want to help all others, especially surgeons, anesthesiologists, intensive care doctors, and others who are at high risk of experiencing trauma and PTSD. Dealing with unanticipated patient death, massive bleeding, adverse outcomes, litigation, and other challenges, can destroy our "identity", and ability to cope and heal.

I was an avid tennis player from sixth grade through the end of high school and played competitively for my high school team. After going away to college and all subsequent years as an adult, I was only able to play intermittently and rarely. Since 2017, I started playing tennis every weekend and it became the highlight I looked forward to every week. By 2019, I started having right shoulder pain and received intermittent injections which helped. In April of 2021, on a typical Friday performing scheduled surgeries, the progressive debilitating pain became so bad that my right arm and shoulder were literally "frozen" in the middle of a sinus surgery. My partner had to come in and help me finish the case. I felt such shame as I couldn't stop crying from the agonizing pain and had to apologize to the parents of that child and then those of the next child. X-rays and MRI later, I underwent shoulder decompression surgery in May 2021 as I hoped to never be in that situation again nor have pain that was far worse than delivering a baby.

After what was supposed to be just a week off of work, and 21 days of rest from performing surgeries, I struggled with severe loss of range of motion and continued to severe pain. I went back to work and performed surgeries as usual, in complete denial as I simply didn't understand what I thought would "fix" the problem didn't. I struggled for almost two years to regain normal range of motion for my shoulder. Six months after the shoulder surgery, I also noticed severe pain first, then numbness and tingling, in my right index finger then parts of my right hand. The most scary were these rare episodes where my hands would look gray like that of a corpse, all from the degenerative discs and bilateral compression and spinal canal narrowing as a result of the degenerative discs in my cervical spine. MRI showed my right C5-C6 cervical spine nerves were the most affected, explaining the symptoms I was having. With more MRIs, cervical injections, and consultations with neurosurgeons and orthopedic surgeons, denial was the only way I could accept my reality. Finally, by December 2021, I activated short-term disability at the end of a busy clinic day, tired and in pain, I simply became desperate and feared what could become worse. It was obvious now that for the past six months, the once-a-week physical therapy at 7–8 pm at night, after 1-hour drive each way to a satellite clinic seeing patients all day, was not enough to help me regain range of motion or function of my shoulder anytime soon.

Taking leave and walking away from work, and the long list of patients waiting for appointments and surgeries, was the only way I could make time to see a chiropractor, physical therapist, massage therapist, or mental health counselor, and undergo daily and weekly scheduled cervical spine decompression therapy and go to the gym to rebuild my now atrophic and weak rotator cuff muscles.

Surgeons are trained to separate our minds from our bodies, through pain and discomfort, and always work as expected by all others. I am amazed in hindsight but understood why I worked using compensatory methods, despite my disabled body. There was so much pressure on me as a physician leader as several members of my team were laid off due to the financial impact of the pandemic. Every physician reading this book will understand how difficult it is for us to ever make a decision that would negatively impact patients, colleagues, hospitals, or the system against expectations and work demands. This is the reason for stories shared among surgeons and anesthesiologists about working while sick, having an intravenous fluid, and various scenarios when clearly the physician should have been sent home or stayed home because of their own illness.

For over a year, I couldn't sleep on my right side due to severe pain with any pressure and lived with pain every day. For about eight months, I wondered every day what it would take and feel like to not have constant pins and needles in my fingers and hand. I remember the first few moments when I stopped feeling the numbness and tingling and wondered if I was imagining that and simply "crazy" because I wished it so.

By the time this book is published, I would have finally returned to clinical work and resumed my career as a surgeon. I am so grateful for these past three years despite the darkness and pain, physical and emotional. Learning that years of poor physical ergonomics as a surgeon has allowed me to collaborate with those with expertise and interest in ergonomics, and now speak on this subject to increased awareness and inspire prevention". Taking medical leave, then walking away from all that I ever knew, spending the past 18 months healing, reflecting, writing, speaking, and giving myself a chance to live without every minute being scheduled or being "late", has allowed me to connect my body to my mind and HEAL in a way that I know I am ready for the rest of my life and career.

I have completed formal courses on physician wellbeing, am a certified trainer for human performance energy management, and have read many articles and chapters voraciously, and listened to podcasts on this topic. What I have not heard discussed, and want to call out, is the reality of the "invisible tax" paid by physicians and their loved ones. The "*tax*" is paid through erosion of physical and mental health, relationships, psychological trauma, ethical, emotional, and moral distress, restrictive covenant (noncompete) policies that prevent a doctor from working when they are able and patients need them, among countless other ways decisions made for doctors and the risks we face, that have been unique to this profession.

I wrote this book not only for physicians but also for anybody who has doctors in their lives. If you have a parent, child, spouse/partner, grandchild, sibling, uncle, friend, neighbor, or colleague, who is a physician or training to be one, or if you are a patient who depends on a doctor or many, I hope you will read this book and get a copy for these doctors to help them achieve the greatest personal, professional, and psychological safety and wellbeing.

Chapter 2

Physician Safety

While healthcare culture, focus, and national headlines across the US have been on "patient safety", the continual rise of "physician burnout" begs the question, *"Are patients safe if the doctors aren't?"* Before I dive into what makes physicians feel "well", and experience "wellbeing" in their daily work, allow me to share the statistics and data on the epidemic of physician burnout.

A study published in *JAMA* (Health Forum) reported almost 50% of clinicians in the US reported feeling burnt out over the past three years.[1] Over the past three years of the pandemic and by the end of 2021, burnout rates reached the highest levels ever at about 60%.[1] Unlike pre-pandemic surveys which showed electronic health records (EHR) as the top cause of physician burnout, this study showed "high stress", followed by "poor values alignment", and "poor work control" as the top factors related to burnout. Furthermore, only 37% of those who felt "valued" reported feeling burnt out compared to the 69% who did not feel "valued". As burnout increased and job satisfaction decreased, there was a direct correlation to a doctor's intent to leave the practice of medicine, which grew from 24% in 2019 to more than 40% in 2021 and likely continued to increase.

Dr. Vivek Murthy, our current and past Surgeon General, declared that confronting the long-standing drivers of burnout among our health workers must be a top national priority. He emphasized that COVID-19 has been a uniquely traumatic experience for the health workforce and for their families, pushing them past their breaking point.

While physicians are gifted with experiencing the beauty in how we heal and restore human health, they are equally impacted by the trauma from grief, loss, and sharing in devastations endured by patients and their families. Through this book, I hope physicians will give themselves permission to be human. Our vulnerabilities are not because of the historical false narrative of "weakness" or somehow being "less than" a "stronger" doctor. Instead, doctors can focus on what is within their control vs system-imposed injury inflicted upon doctors due to our US healthcare system influenced by political agendas and lobbyists, capitalistic incentives, a culture prioritizing margins and financial targets despite knowing the costs to those who directly deliver that care. Doctors have long focused only on mastering the practice of medicine and surgery and unaware of occupational "hazards" and human "hazards" that can hurt us.

By taking systematic actions during medical school, residency, and fellowship, *before* transition to practice, physicians can create personal and professional wellbeing immediately and long term. Faced with unpredictable risk of litigation, disability, divorce, terminal illness, personal tragedies, loss of loved ones, depression, loss of employment, and other risks now including violence from patients, physicians need a network of other professionals to keep them safe. Psychological safety is achieved by planning and creating a network of experts "on call" and available instead of waiting until any "crisis" occurs. I have learned what is required to get physicians to give themselves permission to ask for help, and the kind of help that is most effective. Without which, we are all helpless bystanders for those who ultimately take their own life when physicians believe there is no help or hope possible, nor relief from the immense pain and suffering they endure, not necessarily because they no longer want to live.

Patient safety is impossible without physician safety. What does it mean to have "*safety*" or be "*safe*"? Merriam-Webster dictionary defines "safety" as a noun:

> The condition of being safe from undergoing or causing hurt, injury, or loss.

"*Safe*", as an adjective means:

1. *Free from harm or risk*
2. *Secure from threat of danger, harm, or loss*
3. *Affording safety or security from danger, risk, or difficulty.*

How often do we read headlines or discuss physician "safety", outside of reporting on actual gun violence that occurs in medical care settings? Every medical student, resident, fellow, and physician can use checklists to make sure they know what actions they can take independently from their employers, to create protection against personal and professional risks related to being a physician and being a human.

Regardless of the types of doctors anyone goes to, whether the patient has insurance or not, the co-pay amount, or the office or hospital setting where care is received, patients and their families expect a great experience where the doctor focuses ALL his/her/their attention on the patient. Patients want to find out "what's wrong" or "why" are they having these symptoms. What tests, medications, and/or surgical procedures will be necessary? And does the doctor know what the best treatment plans are to "fix" their medical problems so they can go back to their busy lives?

No one goes to medical professionals to talk about the doctors of course, even though doctors may also possibly be a parent, child, sibling, friend, spouse, and worse, a patient themselves! The idea that doctors are also humans with the same biological and emotional needs, risks, and challenges in their lives just like everyone else, is simply not how society nor patients are asked to think about or know unless the doctors share.

So who is expected to do that for doctors? Other doctor(s) right?

A doctor's job and their only job should be to focus on the patient and no one and nothing else. I am pretty sure nearly every doctor goes to work each day focused on their patients and the countless tasks necessary to do their best for every patient. Years of training to provide as close to "perfect" care as society and patients expect, doesn't guarantee perfect health and outcomes for every patient every day. Doing their "best" despite whatever is going on with their own bodies and their most cherished relationships outside of work, they struggle against daily erosion of their own wellbeing in all domains: physical exhaustion, and emotional and mental health. Physicians must manage their own stress, grief, and loss in both their professional and personal lives while trying to maintain laser-sharp focus. No matter what's going on at work and/or at home, physicians are expected by others, and demand of themselves, to BE "perfect" and not make any mistakes. To experience wellbeing, physicians like all others, must have good physical, mental, emotional, and spiritual health not necessarily in the religious sense, but living in alignment with their core values and beliefs.

CHECKLIST 2.1   WHY PHYSICIAN SAFETY MATTERS

- Just like being a passenger on a plane, in a car, train, or boat, we depend on and expect the pilot, driver, conductor, and captain to be mentally and physically WELL so that our safety is not at risk.
- Physicians who are "safe" can focus their best attention on the patient.
- No one wants to see a doctor with poor mental health or personally physically sick.
- Every patient and their loved ones expect and even demand that the doctors making health decisions for them and with them are healthy so that they can perform their "duties" and not put patients at risk intentionally or unintentionally.

- No patient nor their loved ones want to see a doctor under the influence of alcohol, drugs, medication(s), or with acute health issues that will interfere with their ability to function at their best. We expect all professionals to think, perform, make, and execute the very best decisions for any patient at all times. No exception.
- No patients, if they were aware and could choose, would want to undergo surgery by a surgeon who is not at their best, including being exhausted, sleep-deprived, hungry, or distracted by their professional or personal life crises, divorce, death of a loved one, any variety of issues that humans all face but we expect doctors not be affected by such.
- Doctors are humans with the same or frankly, greater risks for their physical, mental, and emotional health because they are exposed to and endure human suffering while caring for other humans at their most vulnerable state during acute and chronic illnesses, including acute unexpected life-threatening illnesses or traumatic events.
- Every year, over 400 physicians commit suicide. For every physician who dies by suicide, the estimate is that close to a million patients will be impacted directly and indirectly.
- For every physician who commits suicide, this impacts their loved ones and colleagues. Loved ones and family members of doctors who commit suicide are more likely to commit suicide.
- Physicians who are "well" and experiencing high levels of wellbeing are far more likely to work to their highest capacity cognitively, physically, emotionally, and with high levels of engagement. Patients who experience such physicians will enjoy the interactions as a more caring and positive experience.
- A frustrated, exhausted, angry, and unwell physician is far more likely to be disengaged, distant, impatient, distracted, and not demonstrate great listening nor ability to serve patients and make the best decisions with the patient about their health. Instead, physicians may be focused primarily on getting through their day, spending energy suppressing negative emotions and thoughts as they are taught to but exude negative energy unintentionally.
- The physician is expected to be a leader of the entire care team, and their wellbeing, or lack of it, will come through in their mood, behaviors, word choices, body language, and overall demeanor. This can directly influence the dynamic of the care team that he/she/they lead, and further erode the wellbeing of others and the entire team.

- A physician who is using alcohol, drugs, medication(s), or other unhealthy methods of coping with stress from personal or professional challenges, is at risk to self and others. Just like pilots, attorneys, truck drivers, and other professionals whose works impact the safety and wellbeing of others, humans can hide their struggles and still appear functional at work. Until it's discovered, sadly after negative consequences or injury to self or others occur, not paying attention to patient safety and wellbeing poses significant risks to all.
- Any physician who is threatened, unsupported, and unable to navigate challenges or circumstances at home or at work, probably believes that he/she/they can't prioritize their own needs, with an inner voice of "I don't have time". Without intentionally creating time and space away from serving others, the ability to navigate and get help for whatever their needs are, physicians will continue to work every day and live in denial as going to work is far more certain and clear, and gives a sense of "control" compared to addressing challenges without clarity.
- In general, physicians are altruistic, caring, and compassionate. They are masters at taking care of others but rarely themselves. Just as you would likely drop everything to come to the aid of a loved one, friend, or neighbor in need, you would be able to help a physician because doctors are the people most unlikely to ask for help. This is why creating "safety" in every way possible for a physician, through creating a network of professionals that support them, as well as having others understand risk factors to physicians, will help increase the chance that the physician will receive the help they need when they need it.
- Just as we should wear helmets if riding bicycles or motorcycles to prevent head injury in an accident, seatbelts while in the car and when instructed on airplanes, make toddlers and young children wear life preservers when in the water, safety is not an option or luxury IF we absolutely want to avoid risks. Physicians need multiple "seatbelts" at any given time, even when not in the car.

Chapter 3

Data on Physician Burnout and WHY

Why are so many US physicians leaving the workforce? A top reason for many years according to Medscape's annual physician burnout survey, and other research cited the unfulfilled promises of the use of electronic medical records. What was supposed to be the panacea of improving patient safety, care coordination, increasing efficiency, increasing information accuracy, decreasing costs, and other benefits, instead became a high-cost platform used for billing and coding, exhaustive labor, and invisible "tax" on doctors who spend 2 hours typing for every 1 hour of seeing patients.

"The public and patients are often unaware that when not seeing patients in clinic or performing surgeries, doctors have endless and countless task that require their attention every day outside of clinical hours. Notably, "pajama time" (nights and weekends) spent on the computer to complete patient encounter notes, answering nurses questions, patient calls, replying to hundreds of messages from everyone including other doctors and clinic staff, all require time in addition to their busy daily work hours." So, instead of spending time with loved ones or taking care of themselves through exercise, sleeping, or simply relaxing. Electronic Health Record (EHR) was created and used primarily as a billing and reimbursement platform, at a tremendous cost to physician wellbeing and patient experience.[1]

Everyone, not just doctors, should be familiar with data on physician burnout and understand the many factors from the realities of their work environments, job, patient, and employer-imposed pressures today. Until we question what we are doing to protect current and future physician workforce which is

DOI: 10.4324/9781003452478-4

rapidly shrinking against a growing percentage of sicker and aging patient population, the adoption of checklists may seem optional.

In a survey conducted by researchers from the American Medical Association (AMA), the Mayo Clinic, Stanford University School of Medicine, and the University of Colorado School of Medicine between December 9, 2021, and January 24, 2022, it was found that, overall, 62.8% of physicians had at least one manifestation of burnout in 2021 compared with 38.2% in 2020, 43.9% in 2017, 54.4% in 2014, and 45.5% in 2011. These trends were also found to be consistent across nearly all specialties.[2]

Dr. Christine Sinsky, the vice president of professional satisfaction for the AMA highlighted the shocking trajectory of physician burnout from a study by Dr. Tait Shanafelt from *Mayo Clinic Proceedings* published in September 2022.[2] By the end of the second year of the pandemic:

- Mean emotional exhaustion and depersonalization scores were higher in 2021 than those observed in 2020, 2017, 2014, and 2011, increased by 38.6% and 60.7%, respectively.
- 62.8% of the 2440 physicians who completed this survey study had at least one manifestation of burnout in 2021 compared to 38.2% in 2020, 43.9% in 2017, 54.5% in 2014, and 45.5% in 2011.
- Satisfaction with Work–Life Integration declined from 46.1% in 2020 to 30.2% in 2021.
- Mean scores for depression increased by 6.1%.
- 63% of physicians reported some degree of burnout in 2021, a significant increase from 38% reported one year prior at the end of 2020.
- Number of physicians who would choose to be a physician again dropped from 75% to 50%.
- A study of over 20,000 physicians in *JAMA Health Forum* identified control over work environment as a key factor associated with burnout, with 75% burnout reported by those who rated having low "control".
- Lack of control, recognition, and appreciation along with chaos are drivers of increasing rates of burnout.
- One in three physicians plan to cut back on their work hours, which will reduce patient access even more.
- One in five physicians is now indicating they plan to leave their practice within the next two years. One reason for unsustainable overwhelming tasks is the increase in patient portal messages by up to 157% than in pre-pandemic levels, often not requiring physician expertise.

- Physician burnout costs over 5 billion every year by conservative estimates.
- Physicians who are experiencing burnout make twice as many mistakes compared to when they are not.

The AMA is creating an "inbox reduction checklist" as part of their STEPS Forward program, which is a collection of strategies designed to help physicians address and improve workflow and EHR efficiency, billing/coding, and practice management tools, to save physicians time and increase physician satisfaction.[3]

Linzer et al. reported the top four factors identified, using multivariable regression analysis, four factors related to physician burnout: high stress, poor values alignment, poor work control, and poor teamwork. Interestingly, excessive home use of EHR was the lowest factor when ranked by adjusted ratio.[4]

Medscape, the leading online global website that provides access to medical information and education for physicians and health professionals, publishes an annual physician burnout and depression report. As of January 2023, 53% of physicians on average (ranging from 33% in dermatology to 60% in emergency medicine) reported they are burned out, compared to 42% in 2018 prepandemic. Today, 23% of physicians report experiencing depressive symptoms and feelings compared to 15% five years ago.[5]

While data on burnout show an increase for both genders, women consistently experience higher burnout compared to men, 56% vs 41% recently. Yeluru et al. reported gender-specific risk factors for female physicians and possible remedies at the workplace, at home, and specific to their physical and mental health.[6] Unequal pay, lack of mentorship, limited leadership opportunities, time constraints, increased childcare, and household responsibilities relative to male counterparts, childbearing, increased maternal age, and mental health are all factors that increase the risk of burnout for women. By listing these risk factors, the authors can provide concrete suggestions for reducing burnout risk for female physicians such as closing the pay gap, providing early career clinical leadership training, work schedule flexibilities, onsite daycare, transparent advancement policies, improved maternal leave policies and easy access to mental health as key examples.[6]

With so much data, reporting, and research findings consistently highlighting top factors correlated with increasing rates of physician burnout and specific gender-specific factors, what are hospital executive leadership, administrators, and health systems doing to address the burnout epidemic?

There are numerous books written by physicians of various specialties, primary care, and subspecialists, on the topic of physician burnout. Most physician authors, like me, have been inspired to write a book due to personal experience with a high degree of burnout, and/or have had academic interests and research on the topic. Writing such books can be cathartic, intended as a warning for our colleagues and future physicians in training. In fact, in addition to becoming an author, countless physicians have reinvented themselves to become physician coaches and speakers on this colossal epidemic impacting both the physician workforce and the patients we serve. I continue to be amazed that despite repetitive and voluminous headlines on physician burnout, intensified by now nursing and healthcare staff shortage crisis, most of the time when discussing with neighbors or anyone not in healthcare, the reaction is often a blank stare and even surprise.

Ironically, the year before I suffered medical disability, I had worked with HR in my last organization to create clarity for every employee and manager, including physician leaders, on how to take a leave of absence for ANY reason. More on this topic in Chapter 4. See also Checklist 4.5 on what physicians should know about various types of leave and how to take leave. On an early October late afternoon, alone in my office, I picked up the phone and called that number to activate leave and simply did it. No longer worried about how many patients I would impact, how much more burden I would place on my partners and team, and how many surgeries I would not be able to perform, I simply wanted "out". I was exhausted from "hurting", physically, emotionally, and mentally and did not see any light as I was told that surgery may be imminent for my degenerative cervical spine.

After taking a leave of absence for medical reasons under the Family and Medical Leave Act (FMLA) and after I resigned to focus on my health and healing, I devoted my time to my Master in Medical Management program, writing this book, and guest hosted several episodes on Back Table ENT Podcast on topics covered in this book. I also joined several Facebook groups including the incredible national Physician Side Gig with 106K members, the Physician Mom Group (PMG) with 81.3K members, the Physician Nonclinical Career Hunter Group (27K members), and the Female Physician Entrepreneur Group (10K members). Becoming part of these national physician networks allowed me to learn from the daily posts and conversations about pervasive reasons why physicians are leaving the workforce and the various nontraditional, non-clinical job opportunities available.

This has been the most informative experience leveraging social media, as I read about other physician experiences, perspectives, and what physicians are doing to help themselves and each other when they make the gut-wrenching decision to leave the practice of medicine. I am confident very few, including myself, wanted to walk away from patient and clinical care but did so when each of us reached that point of complete exhaustion and highest levels of frustration when our work environments may no longer be acceptable to us.

The universe is intentional, and I am grateful that during the immense stress of pandemic onsent, I applied and got accepted to the Master's in Medical Management program at Carnegie Mellon University Heinz College. My super smart husband Dave helped me with my healthcare finance and accounting classes, and our daughter Claire (high school sophomore then) showed me how to use Canvas to access my coursework and submit homework! After the first four weeks, I realized I never successfully submitted the homework I had completed!

While the program was mostly remote, the few in-person weeks of classes provided such rich learning, from not only the instructors but from my incredible physician classmates from across the US. I slowly gained confidence through learning about health law, health policy, process and variation control, strategy, culture, leadership, power and influence, and critically digital technology and several key topics related to healthcare. As we learned the drivers of the unrivaled increasing costs and expense of healthcare in the US in exchange for the worst life expectancy, without improvement in clinical outcomes, I found myself often angry or in moral distress as we learned how healthcare in this country has been hijacked by politics. There are a multitude of entities whose financially driven incentives and agendas occur at the expense of Americans and their health.

It is not the purpose nor intent of this book to fuel debates or convince readers why universal insurance (not universal healthcare, they are not the same) is truly the single most critical action to decrease cost and increase "health" and access to healthcare for millions of Americans or anyone who lives in the US.

Over expenditure with underperformance is unacceptable for any business or industry including healthcare. Worse, physicians continue to commit suicide at the highest rate in America over other professions. Over 400 physicians die by suicide each year, and suicide deaths are 250–400% higher among female physicians compared to females in any other profession and have a rate equal to that of male physicians. This is not surprising if one is aware that women physicians have higher rates of major depression than age-matched women with doctorate degrees. It is alarming and disheartening that medical students develop high rates of depression within two years of entering medical school, from a baseline of good mental health. Suicide accounts for 26% of deaths among physicians aged 25–30, far greater than the 11% of deaths in the same age group in the general population.[7]

The Physician Foundation, a non-profit focused on supporting practicing physicians, published its 2021 *Survey of America's Physicians, COVID-19 Impact Edition: A Year Later*.[8] Key findings reported include the following:

- Younger (64%) and female (69%) physicians report frequent feelings of burnout compared to older (59%) and male (57%).
- Employed physicians experience more frequent feelings of burnout (64%) vs independent physicians (56%).
- 49% reported reduced income and 32% reported reduced staff due to the pandemic.
- Nearly one-fifth of physicians know of someone who considered, attempted, or died by suicide since the onset of the pandemic.
- While six in ten reported burnout, only 14% sought medical attention for mental health symptoms.
- Eight percent of physicians indicated increased use of medications, alcohol, or illicit drugs weekly because of the pandemic's impact on their practices or employment situation (10% increase compared to 2020).

As a surgeon, I am sadly aware of the fact that surgeons and anesthesiologists are the two specialties with the highest number of physicians committing suicide. What would it take for the American public, lawmakers, policy experts, administrators of health systems and insurers, private equity medical practice owners, hospital board members, and shareholders, to care enough to prioritize and implement broad and comprehensive systemic changes to protect the physician workforce? What are families of doctors willing to learn and do to help their loved one who chose a career to serve others?

In 2019, I had the opportunity to host a documentary screening of a film called "*Do No Harm*", about medical student and physician suicide at the hospital I worked in for our medical students, medical staff, and invited leaders from HR and executive leadership team. I moderated a panel after the screening as we invited the audience to comment and process emotions on this difficult topic. In that same year, I had the privilege of facilitating a contract to have a team of dedicated psychologists who were on call 24/7 for first all physicians, residents, and fellows, then expanded to include all advance practice providers (APPs; the term refers to both physician assistants (PAs) and advance practice registered nurses-known as nurse practitioners).

These measures along with the creation of a medical staff health and wellness committee with doctors and APP champions from various units across the hospital and clinics, as well as having physician leaders such as "division chiefs" and "department chairs", meet one on one with a psychologist, helped to create a new culture where there is full "permission" for frontline doctors and APPs to ask for, receive, and quickly get help. Such counseling and support positively impact physicians' mental health, marriages, relationships, wellbeing, and are even life-saving when extreme stress or adverse events occur to any physician or surgeon.[9]

This book was inspired by Dr. Atul Gawande's book *Checklist Manifesto*. In his book, Dr. Gawande explains how checklists can highly increase patient safety. Focused not on physicians but entirely on patients, he explains how the simple idea of a "checklist" reveals the complexities of our lives and how we can deal with them while mitigating risks.

One example highlighted in the *Checklist Manifesto* was the use of the *Surgical Safety Checklist*, which was spearheaded by Dr. Gawande for the World Health Organization as early as 2008. It has been adopted in more than 20 countries, and now serves as a gold standard for hospital operating rooms before the start of any procedures or surgical incisions. Dr. Gawande is a surgeon, and, as such, much of that book is focused on the use of checklists to optimize patient safety. He also provided insights into medical errors and avoidable failures in healthcare, government, the law, the finance industry, and every realm of organized activity. By using checklists, Dr. Gawande made a strong case that striking improvements are possible not only in healthcare but also in disaster recovery and even businesses.

Research data, media and social media, direct observations, conversations, and countless headlines have exhaustively warned America of the escalating public health crisis of a rapidly shrinking and soon inadequate US physician workforce.

There is now a shift to replace the physician workforce with less trained professionals both to cut labor costs and in response to an inadequate physician workforce. What isn't readily available, are standardized, systematic, logical, and actionable, solutions that physicians can access independent of whether his/her/their employer has created dedicated resources to address physician burnout. Currently, 74% of US physicians are employed by health systems or hospitals. Employers should desire and support actions that will increase physician wellbeing and psychological safety, if not for the moral mandate to care about physicians, at least for knowing that the more "well" the physician workforce, the better the financial performance and business case for healthcare.

Research has confirmed that a healthy workforce with minimal turnover will save any hospital and organization millions per year, in expenses related to recruitment, interviews, and onboarding a new physician to replace physician and non-physician departures due to losing the first physician.

By adopting a "checklist" approach, individuals and groups of physicians, and the hospitals and systems that employ them, can better "compete" in the healthcare marketplace. A strong healthy physician workforce will benefit patients, physicians, and other members of the care team, as well as the financial wellbeing of hospitals, systems, academic centers, and organizations that employ physicians.

CHECKLIST 3.1   REASONS TO OPTIMIZE PHYSICIAN WELLBEING AND WORKFORCE: IMPACT ON THEMSELVES, PATIENTS, AND EMPLOYERS

■ Keep doctors from quitting, so patients can see the doctors they know and trust, and have access to both primary care doctors and those highly specialized to care for the most complicated and life-threatening illnesses.

■ Prevent disruption to physician lives and careers so they can focus on delivering high-quality care.

■ Employers of physicians can save millions by reducing costs whenever a doctor quits, and costs and time delays when patients can't see doctors they need while the employer is trying to recruit a replacement, negotiate, pay signing bonus and relocation costs, licensure and other fees, and costs spent training new physicians to join new systems.

■ Physicians who are well may be less likely to require unplanned time off to address their own mental and physical illnesses and decrease patient access.

■ Prevent physician suicide and minimize the devastating impact, including PTSD, on those who lose a loved one that is a physician, including the physician's families, friends, colleagues, communities, students, and patients.

■ Ensure as many doctors as possible, work as long as possible, to serve and care for the rapidly aging US population who are sicker than ever. So many physicians may defer retirement instead of leaving the workforce earlier than planned if they "feel" like they matter and can practice in a thriving and safe environment.

■ Minimize ongoing physician suicides, which devastate their loved ones, colleagues, trainees, communities, and their patients.

■ Re-energize and rebuild a healthy and robust physician workforce critical to leading and reshaping US Healthcare to one that can leverage technology, innovation, and rapid scientific and research findings to increase "health" for all.

■ Ensure the current and future generations of extraordinary young people interested in a career in healthcare, have healthy physicians to model and teach them how to thrive professionally, fulfill intellectual curiosities, and serve humanity.

Chapter 4

Professional Protection Checklist

This chapter is the *longest* so pace yourself, make a cup of coffee, tea, beer, or wine, and get a snack!

I will highlight in this chapter, all that I wish I was taught over 11 years of my medical education and surgical training (4 – medical school, 5 – residency training, 2 – fellowship). Thank goodness that as a second-year ENT resident in 1997, one of my faculty introduced me to the concept and profession of a "financial advisor".

When asked by my faculty if I had one, I felt embarrassed and answered softly, "no". After all, I had just started making monthly income the year prior as an intern, and quite proud I finally can pay my own bills. Frankly, I didn't have any wealth that required an "expert" to manage.

As first-generation immigrants, my father and stepmother worked tirelessly, lived frugally, and saved in traditional bank accounts, and Certificate of Deposit (CDs), and eventually were able to invest in real estate. They did well for themselves and us, despite coming into this country not speaking any English nor any know-how for assimilating into a new culture. My stepmother was an accountant by training, and I remember my parents reviewing our family's and his business finances as a couple. Many times, they sat at our small glass dining table, reviewing every check, receipt, and other aspects of finances that they probably still do today.

Today, many of us use automated bill pay services and electronic mobile banking. I was so pleased that Claire learned to write a "check" in third or fourth grade at her private school. While my parents didn't stash cash under their mattress or

DOI: 10.4324/9781003452478-5

freezer, I knew they were excellent planners, and saved as much as they could. We lived within our means, never indulged in luxuries, vacations, and rarely ate out (usually Taiwanese/Chinese cuisine if we did). My sister nor I knew what a vacation was, and I finally planned and took all of us on one to celebrate Nancy's high school graduation (I am 11 years older than Nancy). But we were never hungry, we lived well, lacked nothing, and always knew that our education was what mattered the most to our parents. Nope. No one I knew, nor I, had a "financial advisor".

Years later, my sister and I realized our parents did have a great relationship and worked closely with a Certified Public Accountant (CPA) who was also an attorney. She helped them with taxes and other services as our father was self-employed during his years as a working adult in the US. But we didn't grow up aware of any professionals who support our family through their expertise.

How would a medical student, trainee, physician, or anyone know or learn who they should have in their personal or professional network if they didn't experience that or observe it in their own parents and caretakers?

The only professionals every doctor knows unanimously, are other doctors!

They know countless other doctors in their hospitals, clinics, and health systems. This is great if they need to navigate healthcare for themselves, and loved ones, or when asked by friends and neighbors about medical issues. However, physicians MUST know many other professionals beyond those in healthcare. Doctors must identify, build trusting relationships, and leverage expertise by other professionals, so that they are protected and can easily seek help when needed.

This chapter has several checklists with explanations of why each type of professional is critical or necessary and should be in a physician's "web of safety".

The first is a checklist of what physicians should think about when considering a new job, or current or future employer. This checklist covers topics and questions to ask when looking for a new job. For young physicians, just finally reaching the "end" of an exhaustive and long journey in training, reaching their "dreams", puts them at risk of under-negotiating as they are busy feeling grateful someone offered them a job. Thus, soon-to-graduate residents and fellows may not be aware nor think of themselves as a valued "commodity" in healthcare today and negotiate aggressively for themselves.

A physician's "worth" is subjective to the employer's realities, i.e., how urgent they are to fill the position, how long they have tried to recruit unsuccessfully their perception of what the candidate's skills are, and how such skills will fill a need or support their strategies.

Three out of four doctors in America are employed today with fewer and fewer owning their own practices. As dozens of interested parties fight to employ doctors, including private equity, academic centers, hospitals (other than Texas and California which by law can't directly employ doctors), medical groups, health systems, Amazon, Google, Walmart, and insurance companies like United Health (Optum Health, their business unit that provides care directly to 103 million consumers), the fight to directly control the physician workforce has created opportunities for physicians to make better and informed decisions when choosing who to "work for" and hopefully consider the best environment and culture that align with their core values. Physicians need to negotiate for much more than just their salary.

CHECKLIST 4.1   WHAT TO ASK, KNOW, NEGOTIATE, AND CONSIDER FROM AN EMPLOYER

Total compensation, not just salary (monetary and non-monetary)

- Annual salary
- Bonus structure ("formula", metrics, categories, i.e., quality, citizenship, productivity, academic/publications, engagement, % of collections, etc.)
- Percentage of salary at risk (performance-based) vs guaranteed.
- Qualification period before bonus eligibility
- Paid time off for continuing medical education (CME), whether as an attendee, presenter, or invited speaker especially if representing an employer
- Annual allowance for CME expenses (travel, lodging, membership dues, journals, meeting registrations, event-specific expenses such as meals, etc.)
- Salary against benchmark specific to specialty, subspecialty, relative to others in group within and in other similar employment structure
- Annual budget or budget for professional development
- Tuition reimbursement and/or assistance
- Physician or executive coaching (mid-career and beyond, accompany leadership roles)
- 401(k), 403 (b), employer matching
- Profit sharing and distribution
- Research stipend
- Commissions for recruitment of others
- Paid time off (PTO), vacation time, sick leave, family leave
- Retirement plans
- Call expectations

- Organization observed holidays with pay
- Moving expenses (cover ENTIRE move, office, home, family, and pets)
- Sign on bonus (structure, conditions, contingency factors, timeline for payment)
- Sabbatical
- Childcare assistance
- Short- and long-term disability
- Who is the vendor for the Employee Assistance Program, Short Term Disability (STD) and Long Term Disability (LTD) policy
- Insurance (medical, dental, disability, life)
- Gym membership or access
- Parking
- Mileage reimbursement for locations outside the "home base"
- Physician ownership in ambulatory surgery centers or other business entities

The above may not be an exhaustive list (29 items), but it's 28 more bullet points than the only one I knew – *salary* when I was near the end of training and looking for my first job.

Base salary is what you are being paid as an exempt employee for your job, meaning one receives a set amount on an annual basis, paid monthly, bi-monthly, versus hourly wages.

Exempt employees are not eligible for overtime pay, hence physicians who spend hours in *"pajama time"* completing charts, in administrative duties, reviewing patient results and care plans, emailing colleagues, coordinating care, answering inbox messages, phone calls, emails, every task that's not possible during actual time spent performing surgeries, procedures, or, when in clinic, listening to patients and examining them, then making best assessments, treatment plans, ordering tests, referring to specialists, writing electronic prescriptions, printing out instructions, answering questions, all with or without various language interpreters, and reassuring patient and all family members, none of this is "paid" time.

When physicians are given offers for their salary, based on *"benchmarks"* used by potential employers, regardless of whether it's a hospital, health system, multispecialty group, private equity, or anyone else, I hope every physician will take some time to contemplate their actual "worth". Consider the countless minutes, hours, days, weeks, and months of every physician's personal life that will be used for work when outside of work settings. What is the price of all that physicians sacrifice, at the expense of their family time and their own wellbeing? What is the cost to a physician against their perceived "worth" to any employer, or themselves? What is the "cost" of infertility, delaying pregnancy, relationships not had or broken, and families not created, due to demands of this all-consuming profession, against the direct and indirect revenue that physicians generate in how medicine and surgery are practiced in the current US healthcare climate and realities?

Total compensation includes *MORE* than money paid to any employee and includes all the other bulleted points and financial benefits included in the employment contract.

CHECKLIST 4.2 ADDITIONAL CONSIDERATIONS BEFORE EXECUTING CONTRACT

- Any intellectual property that should be excluded from employer (existing businesses, personal branding, websites, side gigs, products, innovations, social media presence)
- Malpractice tail coverage
- Restrictive covenant/noncompete clause – how broad, how long, how far, against which hospitals and systems, what type of work is physician excluded from doing, etc.
- Litigation coverage (per claim and in aggregate)
- For future leadership opportunities, is there transparency when positions become available? Are there true fair and equitable opportunities for most if not all, or simply super-secret handshake and closed-door offerings of opportunities to "friends and families" of current leaders?
- Does the organization consistently perform national searches, recruiting firms, and most of all consider internal candidates as well?
- Is the contract fair? Do they only need to give you 30 days to terminate you with or without cause, while you need to give them 180 days' notice?
- Where are the discrepancies in the contract? For salary and/or any benefits when compared to the offer letter?
- What activities should be "excluded" when they are done on a physician's own time using their own resources?
- Should restrictive covenant apply if you are terminated without cause?
- Should your relocation assistance, an incurred expense for taking the job and moving, be repaid if you are terminated without cause? After all, you already incurred the cost of moving.

The above list hopefully highlights for the reader, that you need to find a great employment contract attorney who can review the contract in detail and discuss it with you before you sign. This is a worthy investment you can make to protect yourself. As high as the divorce rate is in the US, physicians shouldn't be naïve and believe their employer will be loyal to them forever, and vice versa.

The next lists will focus on what experts across various professional industries every physician should identify to create a network for their own personal and professional protection. Such a network is above and beyond what their employer will or can provide. While some benefits may be redundant across both checklists, it will be far better than NOT having such a network. Employers are focused on protecting the organization or system as they should, and benefits associated with employment are not customized for physicians and their unique needs. Instead, benefits are typically offered through third-party vendors through the Employee Assistance Program (EAP).

As a part of the human resources (HR) functionality, organizations offer standardized services for employees to receive a wide portfolio of employment benefits, including referral services for managing leaves of absence, legal, financial, or family services, work-related issues, health and caregiver services, substance abuse, and of course mental health and counseling services. Large organizations and health systems typically use a third-party vendor through a contract, to provide all such services to every employee, and not necessarily specific or different for physicians. However, physician needs are often highly complex and require very experienced experts who ideally should have years of experience working with thousands of physicians across various specialties.

The reality is that the advice and actions recommended by a financial advisor will be very different for physicians, than non-physician employees, due to physicians having such high debt incurred during education and training, higher income, and higher earning potential. Finally, employer-based benefits are not only different but usually subjected to federal and state laws which govern entire groups of employees, but not what's the absolute "best" for any individual physician in the context of their own circumstances.

CHECKLIST 4.3   PROFESSIONALS PHYSICIANS NEED TO BE "SAFE"

- Excellent physicians for their own health and that of loved ones
- General Insurance
- Financial Advisor
- Attorney(s)
- Disability Insurance

- Disability Insurance Attorney
- Leave Manager for Employer
- Accountant
- Psychologist/Counselor
- Physician Coaches
- Executive Coaches
- Career Coaches
- A leader you report to that you completely TRUST who has your best interest in mind.
- Several physician colleagues you can count on as friends, who know MORE, have MORE experience, MORE leadership roles, and MORE education/certification than you. A handful of super physicians who can call that would gladly listen and give you their best advice in your best interest.

Physicians Need the Best Doctors for Their Own Health

Find the best doctors in primary care and each subspecialty you may need. Let's be honest, as physicians, we know too much and frankly have the advantage of knowing what we value and look for when it comes to which physicians are "*good enough*" to care for us or our loved ones. We absolutely would want our own physicians not only to be competent but also to have best surgical skills for their specialty and subspecialties, be knowledgeable with up-to-date science-based information, perhaps even have a research background, and be highly reputable in both academic settings, professional societies, and within their communities.

As physicians, we want what our own patients want when seeing a doctor, someone with incredible bedside manners, who listens, talks to, and treats us like we matter and with respect. We want a doctor who is an experienced and even an expert in their field, a fierce patient advocate. We also want to see a doctor, when we are ill, who is a kind, compassionate, excellent communicator, who will patiently answer our questions without being condescending, all the while confident when providing recommendations and guidance, while using shared decision making to ensure we are healthy, regain health when ill, and achieve life longevity.

Physicians know what types of doctors to avoid: rude, not thorough, ill-tempered, arrogant, self-centered, poor communicators, and one whose style and approach are not patient-centered or reflective of shared decision making.

Worse, no physician would want a doctor for themselves who may exhibit explicit bias, poor listening, arrogant, busy rushing, and not listening or addressing our concerns. Ones who remind you that they are the physician and not open to the possibility that they may not know everything, or that you as a patient may bring forward key information and suggestions that may benefit the doctor-patient relationship. Did I say "relationship"? yeah, that.

How should physicians find the best physicians for themselves and their loved ones? Most physicians simply know other doctors in their hospital or work environment. Others ask their doctor friends who is the "best" or hear of reputations as the great ones are equally reputable as the worst ones. One initiative I took on was asking our medical staff (every hospital has one composed of doctors and APPs advanced practitioners including nurse practitioners and physician assistants), which doctors do they see, do they recommend the doctor, and why. I asked those willing to email me the name and specialty or type of physician, and WHY the doctor would recommend this doctor to their peers. This was my own version of "Angie's List" for doctors. After all, given doctors rarely have time, and when they really need a doctor, they too hope to find the best ones for themselves.

My "resource" list was created in hopes of helping so many who moved to Orlando without any family or friends in town, like us, and it's incredibly stressful already for anyone to start a new life without knowing who to go to for medical concerns for self or loved ones. As my list grew, I gave it to every new doctor who joined the hospital and system, and added other resources including dentists, veterinarians, cleaning ladies, even financial advisors, realtors, and childcare options. This list was reviewed and updated every year for over three years until I left the organization, and often appreciated by my neighbors and friends. This type of "support" is what saves doctors time and energy, and ensures they get the help they need to be well so they can return to work and focus on patients.

For all trainees and early career physicians, it is crucial that one starts to identify and build relationships and friendships with incredible colleagues not only within your own division, department, hospital, and institution, but just as importantly *outside* where you are.

I am blessed that by choosing to join professional societies within my specialty of otolaryngology and subspecialty of pediatric otolaryngology, submit and present clinical research, as well as attend annual meetings, I was able to create a national network of colleagues and friends over the past two decades. This created the utmost gift of endless opportunities to reach out for guidance, help, information, and collaborate to accelerate any initiatives, projects, or whatever I was interested in. What mitigates burnout that is not often spoken of is the immense psychological safety of being able to text, call, or email anyone across the US or world, who will respond and offer advice, support, or activate others to help you personally or professionally.

On a similar note, for many physicians, particularly those who are interested in having a component of their career include activities outside their clinical roles and daily "grind", identifying and building relationships with "mentors" within and outside their own specialty and subspecialty is crucial for psychological and total "safety".

General Insurance

General insurance isn't specific to physicians, but one can insure personal articles like jewelry, cars, and physical assets you own. General liability insurance policies cover you and your "company" if you have one for claims involving bodily injury and property damage from products, services, or operations you are specifically involved in. For many physicians who are now involved in "side gigs" or non-clinical and especially remote work, your home office can be covered in case of natural disaster-related damages that impact your ability to work. An umbrella insurance policy is personal liability coverage that provides additional insurance protection beyond the defined limits and coverages for existing insurance like homeowners and auto insurance.

To have umbrella insurance one must own a standard home, auto, or water-craft policy first. Usually, this is for those who possess considerable assets or engage in activities that could increase the risk of being sued. One can easily argue that being a physician, especially those practicing in subspecialties that typically have high rates of litigation, it's important to find out how to protect your personal assets and those of your family from professional malpractice. Not all states have robust tort reforms that protect physicians or are favorable to physicians against frivolous lawsuits based on perception, speculation, or nonfactual claims.

Financial Advisor

Finding a great financial advisor (FA) may be second in importance to finding a spouse or partner for life. The greatest and most effective relationship is one built on trust, over long periods of time, and someone frankly who has become like a family member to us. I was lucky enough to have met someone incredible during the second year of my ENT residency, who set me up with my disability insurance.

During the first decade of my career, through a recommendation by a fellow faculty, we met and used someone who turned out not to be so great as self-promised. I will never forget the nightmarish day when my husband read online that the "company" this FA represented was going out of business. He called the advisor to find out where our "money" was. All of our savings and investment portfolio, including our trusts and everything we had set up, were at risk.

For this past decade, after relocating to Orlando, we have been blessed with the most incredible FA who cared for us as if we were his family. He isn't a "salesman". He came to our house faithfully every three months after my work hours at the expense of family dinners with his own. We were fortunate to have an FA who was not only knowledgeable, but humble, aligned with our values, and life plans, and took whatever time necessary to explain and set us up so that we did all the "right" things to prepare for the unexpected; my having to take a pause from clinical care and losing significant salary which was frankly more stress-inducing than my injury and pain. We both had our FA on speed dial, anytime and all the time he answered questions, followed up, and set us a variety of savings plans and "buckets" that protected us long-term. He cared about us the way we physicians cared about our patients. I had no doubt that he had far more affluent clients, but never made us feel anything less than being his most important "client" or customer. The trust and relationship we have with our FA are above and beyond the percentage points for him for managing our assets. May all doctors find someone similar.

Additionally, during my challenges navigating the confusing world of disability insurance, activating a disability claim, and fulfilling all requirements to achieve approval for disability benefits, I am forever grateful to the financial advisor who helped me purchase my original policies over 23 years ago. This advisor was not only knowledgeable but cared enough about me and ensuring I received the benefits we needed, that he reviewed all details of my policies and educated me on what to expect as well as what the terms of the policies entailed. Despite being highly educated as a physician, I certainly didn't read every word and sentence, nor understood what my own disability policies really meant, nor cared, until I became injured and our family relied on the benefits.

Attorney(s)

Every physician should have relationships with at least one if not multiple trusted attorneys. Not just an acquaintance or friend, but attorneys who are both knowledgeable and experienced who can and will provide timely and sound guidance for a variety of physician needs. Just as there are countless "types" of physicians, across primary care and all medical and surgical subspecialties, there are up to 28 types of lawyers!

I learned that the term "*attorney*" generally refers to those with law degrees and practice law in courts, while "*lawyers*" also have law degrees, pass the bar exam, but practice law outside the courtroom. An attorney is a lawyer but the reverse isn't necessarily true. Regardless, the purpose of this section is to inform physicians that in the same way, one would not seek information and treatment plans for cancer from their primary care physician but instead an oncologist or team of cancer care specialists, a physician would not go to a tax attorney to seek help and guidance for navigating being named in a lawsuit for malpractice. All of us know who we know based on the frequency of interaction, hence when rare but potentially devastating and high-stress situations arise that threaten a physician's professional, psychological, and personal wellbeing, he/she/they are likely unable to quickly or easily find the best professionals to help them navigate such difficulties. Psychological safety comes from knowing that whatever "surprises" occur during our day-to-day, we will already know or can quickly access those who know more than we do and can help us in all ways necessary.

CHECKLIST 4.4 TYPES OF LAWYERS AND ATTORNEYS ("*": MOST CRITICAL/RELEVANT FOR PHYSICIANS)

- Estate planning*
- Disability insurance*Medical malpractice*
- Employment*
- Real estate/property*
- Contract*
- Intellectual property*
- Worker's compensation
- Tax
- Bankruptcy
- Finance and securities
- Defense (criminal defense and prosecution)
- Constitutional
- Family
- Immigration
- Personal injury
- Civil litigation
- Toxic tort
- Mergers and acquisition
- Environmental
- Social security disability
- Entertainment
- Government

- Military
- Civil rights
- Digital media and the internet
- Public-interest

Estate planning: As soon as you purchase a home, start family planning, and by the time you have children, estate planning is crucial to protect yourself and your loved ones. Advanced directives are part of estate planning. While difficult for physicians to think about, critical to have in place to ensure control over own life and impact on family.

Employment: Starting with your very first offer/contract, invest in a great attorney experienced in reviewing physician contracts, to review, look for risks, and discrepancies, and ensure you have a complete understanding of the contract. Do not be afraid to suggest specific changes before signing.

Disability Insurance

Every resident needs to have a disability insurance policy in place, preferably their own occupation one *BEFORE* they finish training.

- Disability insurance (DI) is critical in case a physician develops a medically related disability. The most common cause of DI claims is work-related musculoskeletal disorders (WRMSD). Injuries include carpal tunnel, rotator cuff tears, labral tears, cervical spine lower back injuries, cervical radiculopathy, and arm issues.
- Factors that increase the risk of injuries related to surgical ergonomics include female gender, surgical instruments, stools, and prolonged fixed positions with poor cervicovertebral angle, for types of surgical cases, resulting in strain.
- High-risk groups include surgeons of various specialties, interventional radiologists (who wear heavy lead vests/aprons), and anesthesiologists (whose daily work involves using their hands in very specific ways, repeatedly, to mask and squeeze a "bag" to deliver oxygen for every patient undergoing anesthesia and even during wake up).
- For all female physicians, pregnancy loss, C-section, any consultation with a reproductive endocrinologist, or use of assisted reproductive technology (ART) may be an exclusionary clause in any disability insurance. Hence it is critical for female physicians to have the best DI policy in place prior to any attempts for family planning and pregnancy.

Even after paying into disability insurance policy since I was a second-year resident, I was astounded by the insurance company mandating my surgical case logs including all Current Procedural Terminology (CPT) codes, employment verification, tax returns, pay stubs, and countless other documents above and beyond medical records and physician attestations on many forms. There is also confusion between short-term disability (STD) and long-term disability (LTD), and which benefit kicks in when and how much money a physician is entitled to when, based on their specialty, income, employer policies on paid time off.

Disability Insurance Attorney

They are ones that specialize and represent impaired professionals, especially physicians. Such attorneys should have experience and focus on disability insurance contracts, long-term disability plans, *Employee Retirement Income Security Act* (ERISA), employee benefits, and insurance bad faith when insurance companies refuse to pay your disability claim without a reasonable basis for denial. Just as insurance companies often deny tests ordered by physicians. I promise you most doctors don't anticipate they may get sick or injured, unaware of the process, documentation requirements, timelines, and their rights and legal protection when it comes to disability and disability benefits.

Leave Manager for Employer

I was unaware during my entire career of how to take a leave of absence or that physicians would ever do that, short of having a diagnosis of cancer or terminal illness of any kind. I always believed taking any leave applied to anyone else just not doctors. The only leave I experienced was the delightful maternity leave in 2006 but had no idea about FMLA nor did I ask. I was too busy worried about the impact on my productivity, bonus, and patients who were waiting, and without any information or experience, decided with the administrator that I had enough vacation time to take eight weeks off for leave without any change to my monthly paycheck.

Years later, not until I "rock bottom", already in a persistently high degree of burnout, struggling with my work-related musculoskeletal injuries, living in chronic right shoulder pain, compensating constantly so no patient was impacted nor my work demands, how ironic that one evening at the end of the clinic, alone in my office, I picked up the phone and called the number to activate leave of absence which I helped to create by working with HR for almost two months the year prior. This had occurred after I learned from a female colleague who struggled with metastatic cancer and had to navigate leave. As the Chair of our medical staff health and wellness committee which I created, I was inspired by her horrible experience and decided every doctor needs to know how to go on leave. Trying to figure this out while you are fighting cancer, dealing with "fax" numbers, and not having the time it takes to do all this so you can be paid and enjoy benefits you have earned, I had no idea I would benefit from this effort personally.

I met with several HR members to work on how to increase awareness and education for all employees, including physicians, on how to take a leave of absence regardless of reasons and types of leave. I had the chance to meet the single Absence Leave Manager who supported over 9000 employees in this health system in facilitating their leave through a third-party company that manages employee leave. This incredible person taught me about every type of "leave" of absence, medical, military, maternity/paternity, bereavement, sick leave, etc. Doctors rarely take all their vacations and frankly would not know how to take leave nor give themselves permission to take leave.

Find out who is the leave manager in your organization or employer. Set up a meeting to understand your state's policy as well as employer policy and the steps required to take planned or unplanned leave of absence.

The ONLY way for a working physician to completely, generously, and effectively devote the necessary time, energy, and effort, receive professional support, and fully engage in activities that will address their own health and wellbeing, regardless of physical, psychological, or emotional (often all three are involved), fight illness, recover from traumatic events, grieve the loss of a loved one, or simply to take a "time out" for the first time or not in their careers, or just to get away from the workplace setting where the trauma occurred. I am confident nearly all doctors unless they have experienced or absolutely needed to take a leave of absence, have no idea HOW to activate and request a leave of absence. They also don't truly believe such benefit applies to them given the immense pressure to serve their patients and meet the pressures of work demands for clinics and surgeries that have been scheduled fully for weeks and months to come.

CHECKLIST 4.5   WHAT EVERY PHYSICIAN SHOULD KNOW ABOUT TAKING LEAVE OF ABSENCE

- When a physician develops a serious health condition
- The birth of a child, adoption, foster care

- Care for your parent(s), dependent child, spouse, or partner with a serious health condition
- Family and Medical Leave Act (FMLA) is a federal law that entitles eligible employees (including physicians) to take up to 12 weeks of unpaid, job-protected leave in a 12-month period. Length of leave may be determined based on length of service and hours worked for your employer. In addition to FMLA, there may be state or local applicable leave laws that may allow unpaid leave and job protection for specific circumstances that qualify.
- Types of leave include family and medical, military, personal, education, short-term disability, and American Disability Act (ADA) accommodation.
- FMLA can be intermittent, continuous, or reduced schedule.
- Find out who your employer uses as a third-party "vendor" that manages leave for them.
- Call the third party as soon as you think you may need a leave.
- Communicate early and frequently with your immediate supervisor (division chief, department chair, senior partner of your practice group, whoever is in "charge" of your practice or who you report to at work) to inform them of your leave status including request. Inform them of the anticipated time you need to be away from work. PS – as soon as you activate leave, your "immediate supervisor" will receive a notification so you should tell them ahead of such notification.
- Be sure to look for communication provided by the third-party leave management service and make sure you complete all tasks asked of you in a timely fashion so that your leave is approved, processed, and managed appropriately.
- Report intermittent FMLA absences to the third-party leave manager and your hospital/organization's leave manager within 24 hours of the absence.
- Your organization's leave manager can guide you on this process if you are unfamiliar with the third-party service they use.
- You can track the process of your leave status and manage your leave, including changing dates, changing from Short-Term Disability (STD) to Long-Term Disability (LTD) leave, and how much FMLA you take using your employer's self-service portal.
- Confirm with your employer's leave manager what you can expect to be paid during your leave, especially for those whose employer policy may cover only a percentage of your salary during leave but you may be able to supplement the rest using banked "hours" or "PTO".

- Anytime you have concerns, issues, or questions, always contact BOTH your employer's leave manager (if you work for a hospital, health system, or organization) and your case manager. Always keep in touch with the case manager assigned to you for the third-party leave manager. For any leave that is related to medical disability or health issues, and even work-related injuries, you must focus on requirements and documentation that they expect and must have to process and support your leave.
- For STD there is an "elimination period" or "waiting period". The first seven continuous calendar days from the start date of the STD. Partial days of absence are not included. STD pay starts after the elimination period.
- For planned leave such as upcoming elective surgery or maternity leaves, you should initiate leave no earlier than 30 days prior to the start of your leave.
- You may not be assigned to the same case manager but I would make sure you have a name, email, and direct line so you can be in contact as needed with the third-party leave vendor as well as your employer's leave manager.
- If you are too sick to complete the necessary paperwork, you can assign a designee to help manage your leave of absence,
- STD only applies to the disability period of a maternity leave which is usually the first half of the leave. The last 4–6 weeks of the 12 weeks of FMLA are considered bonding time with the baby and are not STD-eligible.
- Check with your employer to see if they allow use for PTO when FMLA and/or STD benefits are approved, ultimately especially for female physicians, you have options depending on how much you want your salary to be covered during leave.
- Your benefits should continue uninterrupted while you are on leave as long as you are employed.
- If your disability extends beyond 13 weeks and you are enrolled in voluntary long-term disability coverage during open enrollment with your employer, you will be eligible to apply for LTD benefits which are managed by the insurance company that your employer uses. The third-party vendor your employer uses will usually assist with referral to the right contact person at the insurance company.

Accountant

Given higher earnings, and now more physicians aware of creating investment portfolios, having savings, and being more likely to be in relationships with another physician or high earner, having a trustworthy and excellent accountant is crucial. Finding a great accountant is no different than finding a great physician. We recently changed to someone who listens, takes the time to explain, and was outstanding in how information and decisions were shared with us, especially during tax time.

There are several reasons every physician should find an extraordinary accountant who is experienced, capable, and most of all an excellent communicator who is responsive and expert on tax law. First, physicians are often married to other physicians, and as a couple enjoy high income relative to most. Getting sound advice to ensure appropriate tax withholding to minimize penalties, understanding that most deductions won't apply to physicians, and simply having an accountant file on a timely basis and provide clear explanations for the tax returns filed on behalf of the physician, are crucial.

Second, as more and more physicians leave the practice of medicine, and either change professions, increase investments, and/or engage in "side gigs" and additional and variable income sources, one must have a great accountant to keep track of and ensure appropriate accounting for what can become complex for filing state and federal taxes instead of the traditional reporting based on a single W-2 from an employer.

Third, I could never have expected nor planned that during my "transition" in employment due to disability, loss of identity as a physician/surgeon, and loss of income, my husband would be laid off as well further losing our family's income. Given such drastic changes in our financial status, I engaged in various types of work that were income sources, including becoming a part-time adjunct faculty (instead of volunteer status as in 8 prior years) with formal teaching and advisor roles at the medical school, working as a subspecialty advisor for an ENT locum company, accepting speaking engagements with honorariums, doing contract work with medical equipment/device companies, reviewed medical cases for law firms, and editing for DynaMed a clinical decision support platform that provides evidence based information to health care professionals.

I navigated all the above while creating and launching my physician coaching business, as well as maintained the LLC my husband and I set up 10 years ago that focused on pediatric health. Physicians may face unanticipated disability, inability to work, and losing financial security, as I have endured for almost 20 months while writing this book. My gratitude is beyond description to have been able to resume my career as a surgeon and role as a physician leader. As none of us can predict the future, physicians can't count on the personal and professional security enjoyed today as a guarantee for the remainder of their careers and lives. May my husband and I never lose our incredible accountant.

Psychologist/Counselor

Having easy access and establishing a good relationship with a great psychologist, psychiatrist, or mental health counselor is not applicable to physicians ONLY in private, and only relevant to their personal lives. In fact, most physicians require mental health support due to system-related issues, prolonged cumulative moral distress related to being unable to adequately address all their patient's needs as well as the cumulative sharing of patients' emotional and physical distress related to their disease states. Furthermore, physicians live in perpetual frustration due to inadequate resources, tools, and/or ability to provide expected solutions and answers to patient's circumstantial and all related needs not just purely medical and surgical decision making and navigation of our complex health system and care delivery. There is no clear or district separation between professional and personal lives when it comes to trauma, pain, suffering, and the need to process intense emotions that arise from both personal and/or professional events and challenges.

Physicians will continue to be underserved and under-supported for their mental health needs if employers and society see their humanity as "their problem" and not ones they should bring to "work" in their role as physicians serving patients. As humans, we bring our pain and suffering, trauma, and distress, need for support with us 24/7, as all other humans do. Physicians have likely mastered suppressing their emotions, pain, distress, and frustrations over years of training and in a culture where they are expected to live and function that way. Frankly, if that were possible and the reality for physicians, there would not be issues related to the disruptive behavior of physicians, quality issues, personal addiction problems, as well as the most tragic crisis of physician suicides.

I have always wondered if marriages are more likely to be sustained, and rates of divorce decreased, if married couples engaged in routine counseling BEFORE either one or both reach the conclusion that divorce is their best choice or unavoidable. I had the unplanned, unwanted, and unappreciated experiences of going through intermittent counseling first as a medical student and then again as a surgical resident. Both times of undergoing counseling were due to activation of severe depression, because of both chronic then acute circumstantial "breaking points" coinciding with relationship breakups with two different boyfriends. Late in life, I have enjoyed far more positive experiences in both individual and couples counseling. Counseling for me was always intermittently depending on various stages and challenges in typically my personal but also my professional life.

Why was counseling a far more positive experience as an older adult than when I was a trainee? I have gained the following insights for this question:

1. Due to losing a parent early in life, as well as cumulative traumatic experience well before I entered medical school, I have struggled with situations when intense negative emotions, pain, hurt, and experience trigger a sense of loss, betrayal, and particularly relationship instability that trigger lack of psychological safety.

2. During medical school and residency training, I had not yet learned and was so early in developing a professional identity as a physician. Learners are at the bottom of the professional hierarchy of medicine. I trained at a time when I observed in myself and others, and personally endured misogyny, sexual harassment, racial and gender bias, and micro and macro aggression. I was a young medical student who was horrified as I observed implicit and explicit pervasive gender disparity, even abuse by today's standards, specifically in the culture of surgery which was endorsed and legitimized by a few male surgeons in leadership positions. I count myself beyond blessed, and my career has been possible due to choosing otolaryngology as my first rotation as a fourth-year medical student so that I can be a better pediatrician (I would never have chosen to become a surgeon because of what I witnessed as the absolute most horrific experience of being a trainee in surgery).

   The male and female otolaryngology surgeons were extraordinarily supportive, and nurturing and this rotation after six weeks with two incredible male pediatric surgeons, made me realize and bravely choose to pursue becoming a surgeon. As a younger learner, I had absorbed the pain and trauma of other learners in training. One is simply not equipped to narrate accurately but instead can internalize shame, fear, guilt, and a complete sense of inadequacy based on someone else's inaccurate and subjective assessment and personality dysfunction or ignorance. Counseling was critical during medical school as was a course of anti-depressants which helped me stabilize and function so that I could finish medical school and match successfully.

3. As one endures periods of intense trauma and grief, and even when all seems hopeless, most are able to gain belief over time that by simply "hanging on" and enduring negative mental, emotional, and even physical challenges, better days not yet experienced are possible. I am deeply grateful there are countless individuals throughout my personal and professional journey who were supportive, nurturing, and helpful and provided guidance. Such individuals far outnumbered the few that created devastatingly negative experiences and perceptions of what I believed to be the totality of my life and existence in medicine and surgery.

During residency, when situations and challenges arose, I learned that despite feeling as if my world was ending or I couldn't possibly overcome the challenge, an inner voice was always there that said otherwise. Taking action to ask and receive help, is the only way to accelerate transition into a healthier place of existence and feeling. When suffering, one experiences such distorted reality and narration of one's circumstances. This is why to optimize physician wellbeing, effective actions must be taken without waiting for and before times of trauma, tragedies, and severe distress whether personal or professional.

4. Over the past decade as I gained leadership experience, and intentionally increased my opportunities to support not only physician colleagues, advanced practitioners, learners, and all others across various roles in healthcare, I gained tremendous insight into human suffering and what helps individuals "feel" better and regain ability to function at their best in direct correlation with their own wellbeing. Additionally, my opportunities to grow and reflect were immensely amplified when I received approval and institutional support through executive coaching for one year to support a new leadership role as Surgeon-in-Chief.

   Coaching and counseling experiences, as well as hours of informal but intentional times spent with incredible colleagues who are great leaders, all contributed to my understanding and ability to recognize my strengths and areas where I need to be aware of my inner voice and self-narration or interpretation of events and narratives around and about me. The more time I spent thinking about aspects of my past, present, and especially the impact I want to make in my future based on my core values and passion, the easier it became to continue the practice of self-reflection. To be fair and honest, having developed a medical disability and taking a complete "time-out" from the inhuman pace of how I lived my life is the most critical factor that has given me so much insight and chance to "reset", heal, and now move forward in the next phase of my life and career.

5. Counseling sessions should not just be considered when a physician is under acute devastating distress or experiencing the greatest level of depression. The most effective self-reflection, with some objectivity, accurate narratives, and the ability to evolve requires counseling during a time of relatively less stress and trauma. I have learned that dealing with grief, anger, exhaustion, shame, blame, guilt, and surviving traumatic events big and small, personally or by proxy as the physician involved, such experience is all consuming even when actively and successfully suppressed as a physician continues to work clinically per their schedule and routine.

Chapter 5

Coaching for Physicians (by Physician and by Non-Physician Coaches)

Coaches and counselors are *NOT* the same. The most common use of the word "coach" refers typically to sports and someone who trains and organizes a sports team. The broader definition for a coach, specifically when not referring to sports, would be an individual whose professional job involves teaching others so that they may improve at specific skills, topics, and subjects, and/or to help the individual enhance their performance in specific domains.

In medicine, trainees and practicing doctors are far more likely to have experienced and adopt the concept of having a "mentor", instead of a coach. Mentors in medicine are typically other physicians who are older, further along in their career and practice, and have more clinical knowledge, surgical/procedural skills, and experiences as a physician. One simply assumes that when asking another physician defined by such a description, one has a mentor.

Perhaps the confusion lies in that some mentors may be great at sharing how to perform surgical procedures, how to apply for research grants, develop a clinical program, and/or share experiences in dealing with complex or challenging clinical scenarios specific to patient care. Yet one can be a great mentor but not necessarily also a great coach. Sharing one's successes does not guarantee successes in others even if they try to emulate such successes. A coach, in contrast, is

DOI: 10.4324/9781003452478-6

someone who knows the individual well, understands their goals, and then helps the individual being coached reach their goals and potential through asking them reflective questions and helping them live in alignment with their core values and goals. "Mentoring" is a term that typically focuses on professional and career development, coaching may be individual but also team-based with a particular focus on relationships.

Ultimately, any physician may need and will surely benefit from both. However, it is far easier to find "mentors" in medical education and healthcare, than professional and excellent coaches who have specific expertise in medicine. It is even more relevant and rare, to find a coach who is also a physician, that has personally experienced the area of expertise they offer coaching. Such expertise and guidance is simply not readily available through training nor acquired by reading book chapters and articles.

Physician Coaching

A few years ago, I became aware of physicians who switched their career from one of practicing clinical medicine to one where they serve as a "coach" to other physicians. It wasn't clear exactly how a physician would be ascribed as someone qualified to coach another physician. Most seem to comprise primary care doctors, perhaps those who chose to leave the practice of medicine at the peak of their own burnout. These are physicians inspired to create positive change and help fellow physicians, through sharing of insights from their own experience. Some I recognized through reading of their books on the topic of physician burnout. Others, I personally met or heard from their speaking engagements on the topic.

Physicians can now find physician coaches through social media, particularly through Facebook professional groups including *Physician Nonclinical Career Hunters*, *Female Physician Entrepreneurs*, and *Physician Side Gigs*.

I have spoken on the topic of burnout, then shifted to wellbeing, for the past 12 years, as well as been writing on this subject. My talks continue to evolve year after year as I have gained new experiences that inform my understanding of what erodes my own wellbeing and work as a physician and surgeon. Through my master's, I met a nonphysician career coach and decided to work with him when it wasn't clear whether my medical issues would ever improve to the point where I could return to clinical practice nor how to support my family. This uncertainty was compounded by the two-year, 30-mile noncompete restrictive covenant which made potential employers hesitant to offer any employment options. I will never forget the difficulty and frustration of navigating cobra health insurance for my family and I, and often wondered how the lay public deal with the complexities of our healthcare system if I had such difficulty despite being a physician.

In the initial weeks, my career coach and I focused on my strengths, experiences, skillsets, and what I am most passionate about as well as activities that I want to have as a part of any future job and career. After over a decade of informally supporting physicians, both male and female, across various specialties and primary care, I decided to launch a coaching business specific to physicians and offer coaching on what's covered in this book: how to achieve personal, professional, and psychological safety.

It took several months to outline the business plan and details before I officially launched my coaching business. As I was still in my master's, I didn't have time to undertake formal training to receive certification for coaching – but that hasn't stopped many other physician coaches.

Twelve months after launching my physician coaching business with a focus on physician wellbeing, despite sending dozens of emails and service sheets to organizations, individuals at academic institutions whose roles influenced physicians and medical staff, I have had only one client to date.

After much reflection amidst disappointment, I believe there are two likely reasons why physicians do not want coaching regardless of the severity or types of challenges they face.

First, most physicians simply do not believe they need another physician to tell them what is best for them. I belong to a profession where we spent years as medical students, then as residents, and additional years as fellows for those who chose to become a subspecialist; we are taught to continually learn and gain confidence so that we would have the answers to just about everything related to our field of practice in medicine and surgery. We work and live in a culture where we are expected to always know the answer. When we don't, the educational training and journey is such at every level that one is expected to ask those who are further ahead of them in their careers as doctors, or more senior members in their group or academic departments.

The assumption is that those who have worked more years than we have and older than we are, will likely know the answers to the challenges we face in our professional practice of medicine and surgery. This may very well be true, but it's far from adequate. If I am dealing with a complex airway issue in a pediatric patient, of course, I would not hesitate and in fact be quite grateful to reach out to a few colleagues who are renowned for their expertise in my field of pediatric otolaryngology. Such colleagues have absolutely given me great and free advice on how to perform certain types of procedures and to do them successfully, as well as several other pearls that are invaluable. However, such individuals may have never experienced being sued, faced litigation, unplanned patient death, being laid off without cause, or political struggles at work as well as countless other challenges in our professional lives.

While physicians can ask their peers, colleagues, "bosses", and anyone else who is also a doctor, same type or different, for advice regarding financial issues, divorce, and mental health struggles, when it comes to personal and psychological challenges, most physicians are far more likely to keep that a secret. Physicians are only rarely open to sharing their personal challenges with a few highly trusted individuals whom they consider their closest friends as there is such risk and stigma associated with any physician who may be "human" with needs and vulnerabilities. Physicians will ask for advice from co-workers and colleagues who practice the same type or even different types of medicine or surgery, their "division chiefs", or "department chair", or another physician in the chain of command in hospitals and medical centers. What they don't realize is that such individuals may not have the utmost expertise, experience, competence, and abilities to help physicians with their needs when the needs are NOT related to patient care and the practice of clinical medicine and surgery.

Physicians expect to receive advice and guidance from those who work with them, and for *FREE!* This is great for patient-related matters, but for physicians facing their own challenges, I will highlight the many professionals outside of medicine that every physician may need at some point in their careers and lifetime.

Second, physicians are unlikely to ask for help due to the very culture that expects all physicians to always have the correct answer for everyone including themselves. I have observed and it's been validated by many friends, families, and the many patient families who come to me for second or third opinions that some physicians not only won't admit they don't have the answers but, at times unfortunately, they minimize or become dismissive of the patient's concerns and questions.

The sad truth is that Americans will only experience more of this, as the workforce attrition accelerates, and more and more people no longer see a physician but instead the physician assistant or nurse practitioners who may be excellent but can't substitute for the depth or experience of medical and surgical knowledge that physicians possess. The greatest risk to the public is when physicians or healthcare providers tell them non-evidence-based, inaccurate, or false information, then prescribe treatments that might or might not cause harm, but are less effective than they have implied to or convinced the patients. If physicians believed others know how to help them better than themselves, perhaps more would ask for help, seek counseling for themselves or their relationships, and most of all, ask for help from another physician for their own struggles.

The reality is that physicians today can and are, easily asking other physicians for suggestions on how to treat patients and symptoms or suggest ideas for correct diagnosis. How interesting that I see multiple daily posts on Facebook from groups such as Physician Mom Group (an all-female physician group), where one physician posts photos and asks for advice for a variety of clinical symptoms for their patients or themselves and their loved ones. Then countless other physicians in the specialties that treat such issues, will comment, and provide advice.

Bottomline, physicians are likely resistant to "coaching" despite having had coaches in any athletic experiences. Engaging in coaching requires a commitment to scheduling time and committing to the cost of coaching, even if such services are exactly what they need to achieve personal, professional, and psychological safety.

During nearly a decade before my recent period of medical disability and time away from clinical practice, I sought out training in various courses and learning cognitive content on energy management, burnout, wellbeing, system-based solutions, and structured programs that should help all physicians. Of all the activities I have participated in or led, those that allow me to explore and process not only my own trauma, experiences, intense pain, and emotions deeply suppressed for decades, have provided the most transformative changes in my healing and ability to feel strong and resilient.

One specific activity that I am deeply grateful for, is having the chance to guest host several podcast episodes on the Back Table ENT Podcast, on various topics on wellbeing. This podcast was founded by a wonderful physician couple, a dear friend Dr. Gopi Shah, a pediatric otolaryngologist, and her husband Dr. Aaron Fritts, a vascular and interventional radiologist. I created the content of each episode, and such allowed me to meet several extraordinary female physicians who launched their "coaching" business in a specific professional area that they are passionate about based on their own journeys and even traumatic experiences. The year before this book was written, I introduced them to each other so that we may support one another in our tireless fight to help other physicians and trainees. These physicians have all inspired me to continue my journey to create a positive impact, as a physician coach or otherwise.

Here is a checklist and outline of all areas I can support any trainee or physician as a physician coach.

CHECKLIST 5.1   DR. JULIE WEI'S PHYSICIAN COACHING SERVICES

- Medical disability from temporary or life-threatening illnesses.
- Second victim syndrome, including PTSD from adverse outcomes and sentinel events.

- Employment-related risks and challenges, including separation by choice or force.
- Legal matters related to personal or professional matters, including being sued.
- Activating leave and navigating process, for any type of "leave".
- Optimizing employment and HR benefits related to temporary or permanent leave.
- Understanding the importance of disability insurance and how to navigate receiving benefits.
- Negotiating employment contracts and assessing "fit" between core values and one's professional goals in alignment with the employer's goals.
- Risk of or going through divorce and other critical relationship changes.
- Navigating mental health crises, acute and/or chronic.
- Critical conversations and communication for results.
- Creating space, time, and routine for nonwork/self-care, amidst work and life demands
- Addiction.
- Infertility and delaying pregnancy.
- Career/professional development, visibility, advancement.
    - Decisions related to "staying" vs "moving".
    - Increase career visibility within and beyond own organization and specialty.
    - Prioritization of discretionary efforts within/outside the organization.
    - Successful and timely promotion on any track.
- Challenging job-related issues, relationships, performance, barriers to advancement.
- Clinical research: mentoring trainees, research design, manuscript writing, collaborators.
- Creating optimal "productivity" and workflow, maximizing positive experience at work.
    - EHR efficiency (clinic note templates, order sets, smart sets, smart phrases, AVS-after-visit summaries, etc).
    - Clinic Template/Visit Types to optimize RVUs and access.
    - Managing no-shows.
    - "Prepping" for your day.
    - Delegating appropriately.

- Strategic planning for pace, timing, and decisions for retirement.
- Creating your "perfect" day and schedule: Clinic, Operating Room, Admin, Research
- Coaching for greater wellbeing: micro-, macro-actions, and new routines.
  - Exercise and sleep hygiene for self and young children.
  - Nutrition plan for self and family.
  - Protecting non-work time and saying "YES" based on value added.

As a physician coach, I know the best way to help physicians is to ask questions so that they can reflect and articulate their personal and professional "current state" before identifying factors that create erosion of their wellbeing. I have learned not to tell physicians what to do, or how to live their lives, or what NOT to do. I learned from those who have helped me, that by creating space and time for physicians to focus on themselves, they may actually hear their own voices so they can connect with what pains them the most. It's amazing to support someone and help them learn to trust themselves and stop judging their emotions and feelings while regulating their inner narratives. This then can create belief in all the possibilities within one's own control to make changes that improve one's health, wealth, wellbeing, and that of their loved ones as well – regardless of a physician's system or employer.

I have been most blessed to have met and been supported by extraordinary counselors, executive coaches, career coaches, financial advisors, and absence leave managers and know great physician coaches. Having now a network of such professionals and physician coaches, who each used their own pain and trauma, and then spent years creating expertise from these experiences so others may benefit, this is the gift I offer. Such professionals and their expertise when needed, are how we can make sure every physician in need can be "safe". I consider it my "superpower" to be able to connect any physician to my network, regardless of their challenges, so that a physician is never alone and can experience utmost psychological safety amidst a career that consumes our every breath if allowed.

Surgical Ergonomics and Coaching for Surgeons

In October 2021, after five months of hiding my daily right shoulder pain and inability to reach my right arm up past my shoulder, nor zip up my own dress using my right hand and arm, inability to reach anything up high, while having continuous numbness and tingling, my left hand/arm/shoulder became the "workhorse". By Thanksgiving, I had the first of a few episodes where my entire right hand and fingertips would turn bluish-gray, creating much panic in me as the physician in me knew that circulation or something neurological was wrong, likely from the compression of my nerve coming out of the C5-C6 foramen. I had to stay calm despite feeling so helpless while praying and hoping my nail-beds would soon turn pink again. These episodes would occur randomly but last between 5 and 10 minutes.

As soon as I started my FMLA and gained entire days free from scheduled clinical care, I made sure my hours were spent instead on chiropractic decompression therapy for my neck, physical therapy to increase range of motion for my right shoulder, massage therapy for mostly neck and shoulder, and then more time at the gym where I would do exercises taught to me by my physical therapist. In this past year, I learned about the term and topic of "surgical ergonomics". While a patient and not an expert on this subject, "ergonomics" comes from the Greek words "ergon" which means work, and "nomos" which means natural laws or arrangements.

Ergonomics is the study of people at work and how their working environment is designed to suit the worker, which has NOT been the case nor discussed or taught to surgeons and physicians until very recently. Recently several surgeons across various surgical specialties have written about this topic, just as I have for my own otolaryngology colleagues. Such is the ultimate service of a physician, we use our own injuries and experiences, and turn them into public service announcements and warnings for fellow physicians. While I have learned about my own body and my health, and gained a better understanding of my years of repetitive and horrible physical posture while doing my job which I loved. I also learned that my injury stemmed from multiple factors yet resulted from what seemed to be an unavoidable occupational hazard as I fulfilled all three top risk factors to develop Work-Related MusculoSkeletal Disorders (WRMSD): *use of headlight, loupes, and microscope.* Despite not being an expert on human factors, nor an engineer, nor an expert on surgical ergonomics, I have found such an expert who is committed to enhancing awareness, education, and prevention through collaborative research and shared learnings.

Surgical Ergonomic Coach

Dr. Geeta Lal is a board-certified General Surgeon in both the USA and Canada, with advanced Fellowship training in Endocrine Surgical Oncology. Given her own journey with chronic myofascial pain, misdiagnosis of temporomandibular joint disorder (TMJD), and much self-learning, she discovered that she too had developed musculoskeletal problems as has been shared by surgeons across so many other specialties. She has turned her passion specifically into speaking and coaching to help not only current surgeons but especially trainees with future careers as surgeons. Surgical coaching is an important tool for individual surgeons not only to improve their surgical performance through better ergonomics, but critical to support surgeon wellbeing, quality, and safety for patients, and increase career longevity for any surgeons.

Surgical Performance Coach

While I have never served as one by title, I have spent the past 20 years doing what every surgeon who practices in academic settings does: teach medical students, residents, and fellows, and/or help younger surgeons with the art and science of performing surgery and variety of surgical procedures in my specialty and subspecialty. Surgeons do not become "experts" in surgery simply after finishing their residency and for some additional fellowship training for subspecialty.

Achieving mastery as a surgeon requires constant reflection, intent, and focus on "perfecting" each case, case after case over years in one's career. Not all surgeons gain mastery the same way, nor in the same timeline. There are those who are known by colleagues and gained reputable as the "masters" and ultimate "experts" as a surgeon, yet they may or may not also be an expert in teaching excellent surgical skills to accelerate another surgeon to achieve desired outcomes in their own surgical performance. A surgical coach then, is someone who can guide a surgeon to think differently and learn new approaches to their own approach, thinking, surgical actions, and outcomes. A surgical coach partners with a surgeon to receive one-on-one guidance and together as in other coaching relationships, they can set goals and action plans, and gain skills to handle stressful decisions and situations during surgery.

For surgeons who want to become certified surgical coaches or find a surgical coach, the Academy for Surgical Coaching is an independent non-profit founded to provide surgical coaching services to not only individual surgeons but also professional societies and healthcare systems. They use video-based coaching platforms to connect surgeons across institutions nationally and internationally.

Navigating Litigation

I was named in a lawsuit, claiming I caused long-term learning disability in a child whom I performed tympanostomy tubes from eight or nine years earlier in a different children's hospital in a different state, who had a residual "hole" in his eardrum after the tube extruded. The hole and temporary mildest of conductive hearing loss were reversed and corrected after a procedure performed by a colleague as I had left the state and moved to work in my new role, hospital, and health system. Without divulging details which is not the purpose of this section, I want to highlight WHY physicians who experience being names in a lawsuit and worse, undergoing litigation, are best served to have a physician coach with expertise.

First, after decades of watching a few exciting lawyer and legal drama shows such as "Ally McBeal", "Boston Legal", and a few episodes of "Law and Order", I remembered after the initial shock, shame, fear, anger, and having my entire identity shattered because I was made to feel like a horrible physician and surgeon when there was so much evidence to the contrary. Here are some lessons learned through three years of exhaustive experience which resulted in settlement at the advice of my counsel.

Second, I was adamant that I wanted my "day" in court. After all, the jury deserves to know who I am, my career accomplishments, and testimony from experts in my subspecialty across the country. Furthermore, it would be easy to share the countless positive affirming comments about me as a physician and surgeon from various parent/mom groups on Facebook. I was shocked to learn that facts and evidence didn't matter. In my case, I was advised that it would be a huge mistake to go to trial because the county from which the lawsuit was filed had a record of nearly 97% decisions in favor of the plaintiff.

I was educated that despite having evidence and expert testimony which refuted the plaintiff's claim, should I go to trial, and receive a judgment against me, this would be on my professional record forever. I recall months of intermittent rage, anger, sadness, and even depressive feelings, suppressed while working furiously focused on my day-to-day responsibilities, as this case was a shadow looming over my every waking moment. I will never forget the day of the mediation as I sat in my sister's kitchen. I had flown to Oakland from Orlando to help my sister with her newborn and my new niece. For over 4 hours, my attorney negotiated with the plaintiff's attorney until we reached a settlement. I cried for hours despite this settlement and have never forgotten the trauma and toll it took on me during those years.

Physician Coach for Litigation

I wish I had met and known Dr. Gita Pensa who became a physician coach whose expertise is in helping physicians navigate litigation. Dr. Pensa is an emergency medicine physician in an academic center, who turned her own traumatic experience into expertise after interviewing, coaching, and counseling over hundreds of doctors during or after litigation. She created her podcast *Doctors and Litigation: The L Word* exploring malpractice litigation and litigation stress.

Dr. Pensa is an expert physician coach who provides one-on-one coaching as well as group coaching to support doctors facing and enduring litigation and adverse events. As a litigation physician coach, she has immense insights and experience to help physicians navigate the emotions of being sued, and how to process their trauma instead of living in isolation and shame during such intensely stressful times. Having a physician litigation coach will decrease the risk of burnout, shame, self-blame, fear, anxiety, and false inner narratives that are huge factors for suicide. This is one example of how physicians can gain psychological safety and professional support. Dr. Pensa's coaching is not focused on the facts or legal issues of the case, instead, she will help physicians navigate their experience while under litigation to protect their wellbeing.

Career Coaches

It is beyond the scope of this book to provide details or expertise on the topic. The demand for career coaches has increased significantly through the pandemic as so many people demonstrated "quiet quitting" and outright quitting, across various industries due to factors forced by the pandemic and shifts in priorities and values for workers. Physicians have also been heavily impacted. Due to the ever-increasing prevalence of "burnout", loss of control and autonomy, and continued increase to "produce" and perform despite the massive shortage in nursing as well as medical assistants and technicians across healthcare, the younger generation of physicians who have either just finished residency or still in residency, are looking to get out of medicine or pivot from the traditional assumed career of being a "doctor" until they retire.

Career coaches are experts in helping professionals in various or all aspects of their career planning and development, including resume building, interviewing, branding, LinkedIn and social media presence, negotiating, career transitions, objectives, and decisions. Working with a coach is once again the opportunity for intentional reflections, self-identification, and accountability to take actions toward declared professional and career goals in alignment with one's core values and timeline, and hopefully matched by best skillsets and built upon but not limited by past experiences and achievements.

I worked with a career coach, Stefan Werdeger, who founded a career coaching firm based on his passion for finding the right leaders for organizations as an executive search consultant. I had the fortune of meeting Stefan during my master's program at CMU, and it was during my year away from clinical practice, facing uncertainty, that his career coaching allowed me to focus and take actions in preparation for a complete *SHIFT* from a career in clinical practice to one that supported my passion and history of supporting physicians, trainees, and others in achieving greater wellbeing and psychological safety through connecting them to professionals they may need.

Physicians may confuse career coaches with their "mentors", which every physician has simply by identifying any one or several faculty members from their training in residency and/or fellowship. There are clearly differences between getting advice from a mentor when needed, versus an intentional, individually focused, relationship with a career coach.

Executive Coaches

When I had the opportunity to assume the role of "Surgeon-in-Chief" in addition to serving as Division Chief with my past hospital and health system, I advocated for myself to receive financial support for an executive coach. First, there are many out there, and as a physician who had never experienced a career coach, or physician coach, let alone an executive coach, I was aware that executive coaching is highly typical in other industries but when in healthcare typically reserved for C-suite executives or others in higher leadership positions. Thanks to my dear and longtime friend and supporter, Kevin Grigsby, who had served as Senior Director of Member Organizational Development at the Association of American Medical Colleges (AAMC), he knew me well and absolutely insisted I meet Kari Granger, CEO and Founder of the Granger Network.

Kari Granger is an executive coach who focuses on transformative leadership development, and I was humbled by her extraordinary background as a combat veteran in her military experience and leadership working with numerous branches of the US armed forces. My experience working with Kari as an executive coach was extremely powerful and continue to shape my own leadership journey. While I have never been trained nor had experience with the military, there are almost parallels in healthcare, especially in operation rooms and high-risk areas in hospital settings where logistical operations, adverse/sentinel events, natural disasters, or mass casualties situations, all require the strongest of leadership and a culture of trust, collaboration, and accountability.

Chapter 6

Personal Checklist

Work–life balance is no longer the "buzz" word, instead replaced in recent years with "work–life integration" coined by Berkeley Haas School of Business. This was frankly way overdue given that "*balance*" is simply not possible, the time we spend at work far exceeds time spent living our lives outside of work. Time spent on work now includes nights and weekends when we may be home outside the hospitals and clinics but chained to our computers to complete countless tasks that await. Physicians work at least 9–12 hours per day physically away from home and in healthcare facilities, not referring to those who do "shifts" of 10 or 12 hours for hospital-based services such as anesthesiologists, intensivists (doctors who run intensive care units), hospitalists (doctors who works shifts, and take care of patients who are admitted to the hospital and act as "quarterback" who manages their medication, and coordinate tests and consults to various specialists), or emergency room physicians. Most physicians who work full time likely have less than 4–5 hours of personal and family time per day, when away from clinics and hospitals that's not their biologically mandated crucial sleep time.

No physicians I know, including female doctors who felt they had to choose to go part-time to meet demands as mothers/caretakers for children and/or elderly parents, have experienced "balance" when it comes to having "time". While this is not unique to doctors, it's a basic yet significant driver for physician burnout – unrelenting work without adequate "recovery" or rest against physical exhaustion compounded by emotional and mental distress.

Work–life integration describes the approach and framework that creates more synergies between all areas that define "life"; work, home/family, community, personal wellbeing, and health. At least by removing the word "balance",

DOI: 10.4324/9781003452478-7

perhaps physicians can take some solace in feeling inadequate to bear the implied responsibility and inadequacy by not achieving "balance" as if it's up to them. Integration is remarkably an accurate word to describe realities for most physicians. When in the hospital and healthcare setting, most female physicians, and males, can attest to texts and calls from their nanny, children (if old enough to have a phone), spouses, family members, or anyone in need.

Being a physician never protects one from needing to care for others in their lives who are not their patients. After finally getting home, emails and texts from coworkers and colleagues, and completing tasks from the day or days before by logging into their computers, perhaps after dinner and putting kids to bed, and always on weekends, that's a form of "integration" but an unhealthy one. Integration in this context really describes the ridiculous spilling over of "work" and tasks related to patient care and administrative tasks that suck what little "life" or time that is outside of clinical care for most doctors.

The public is likely unaware that every physician employed by a hospital or system is required to complete dozens of web-based trainings (WBTs), on all topics that most other professionals are required to do, except far more and specific to healthcare. For example, doctors must complete training on harassment, diversity equity, and inclusion, billing fraud, Health Insurance Portability and Accountability Act (HIPAA) compliance, patient safety, mass or natural disaster drills and how to evacuate, requirements to minimize contamination due to exposure to patients' body fluids and blood, electronic records documentation, research specific rules and compliance, and many more. Doctors do not get protected time away from patient care to do all these trainings and they must be repeated every year.

Some doctors are also passionate about other contributions besides direct patient care, such as education, research, professional organizational memberships, advocacy, writing, mentoring trainees in manuscript preparations, reviewing journal articles for peer-reviewed research, giving presentations, and many others that contribute to the advancement of the science of medicine, impact public health, and ensuring future generation of physicians who will serve our society. All such, while not direct patient care, requires time.

Time is money as my father always says. Employers often do not protect such time, as a physician's time is usually expected to be used for direct patient care which generates revenue. Some ways for a physician to "buy" their time, is to either be involved in administrative leadership work and/or if they are a funded researcher such that the funding covers part of their salary. The elusive time for physicians who engage in such activities is then found on nights and weekends, stolen quietly before the rest of the family is awake, or from time enjoying personal hobbies. It's not black and white and for each person, it varies across life and even career stages. Those who chose a career working in academic settings typically made less salary compared to those who devote nearly if not ALL their professional time to direct patient care. Regardless of what any physician chooses, or perhaps even transition from one job type and setting to another, every physician must be accountable and take action to ensure his/her/their own wellbeing as defined in a holistic manner.

This chapter highlights several separate personal checklists, all of them focused on the intentional commitment of energy and time when *outside* of any work setting. The personal checklists are based on creating mindset and perspective through repetitive daily actions and activities, or as many as one chooses, to increase physical, emotional, mental, and spiritual wellbeing. Such can be described as "micropractices" or "microactions" for wellbeing.[1] The checklists below should help physicians who live in a constant state of rushing, running out of time and life, learn to be "still" and fully engaged in each moment instead of in anticipation of the next task due that requires completion yesterday.

So many physicians have resigned to believing that they are fine and telling themselves they need to "push through" their life until their next "vacation" when they can get away for a few days or one week. Sadly, for most, it takes 2–3 days to "unwind" and actually be present for their vacation with loved ones and family, then just when that starts to happen, the anticipation of emails and inbox messages, and soon returning to work, creates anxiety to either get on the computer while still on vacation else become preoccupied with dread and counting the days until returning to work.

The science of sleep and research data show just because one does not need to get up at 6:00 am or 6:30 am and has a day in which they can sleep in, the sheer habit, mental stress, anxiety, and schedule changes do not automatically mean a physician is fully resting when they are not working. I have long envied my younger sister (non-physician)'s ability to sleep in when allowed, but also feel guilty that my husband (non-physician) has rarely ever slept in on weekdays or weekends because he is married to a surgeon whose work schedule requires early start each day. After 20 years of going to bed at the same time and getting up at the same time, we at least enjoy more early morning coffee time on weekends and during vacation days.

As for which activities and elements of physician home life can be (or should be) outsourced, particularly for female physicians, here is a separate checklist for such so that one may reclaim both time, life, and sanity. Every decision has a cost, direct or indirect, financial, or emotional, and provides a different experience for the physician and their family. The most important achievable goal that supports wellbeing is the opportunity to empower oneself to make decisions based on facts, needs, and what will decrease physical, emotional, psychological, and visceral feelings of exhaustion with no hope in sight as in a few hours the day starts again.

CHECKLIST 6.1   DAILY "MICROPRACTICES" TO INCREASE POSITIVITY AND WELLBEING

▪ Every morning, as you get ready, look in the mirror and smile at yourself. Say out loud "I love you" and wish yourself a GREAT day.

▪ Say "hi" to anyone you walk past, or when in an elevator, with a smile and eye contact.

▪ "Walk as if you are kissing the Earth with your feet" – Thich Nhat Hanh.

▪ When asked, "How are you?", pause then say exactly how you feel: "Not sure", "good", "okay", or "great", or name other emotions, i.e., "happy", "excited", or "worried".

▪ Don't ask others how they are unless you care and are willing to STOP and listen.

▪ When interacting with others, observe their stress and energy levels. Offer calmness, slower speech, and positivity, and watch yourself create a SHIFT in others' moods and emotions.

▪ Commit at least one act of kindness.

▪ Give a heartfelt compliment to a loved one and someone at work.

▪ As soon as visceral feelings of anger, anxiety, frustration, or discomfort are observed, find a space nearby, and walk away from the person or surroundings if possible. Find a window, look out, and take three long slow deep breaths or more.

▪ Say "thank you" sincerely and specify for what. Say it frequently.

▪ Listen to your favorite songs during drive to work and on the way home.

▪ After pulling into the garage, before going into the house, pause and think about what you want your evening to be. Decide what you will not repeat about your day.

▪ When walking in after work, immediately hug and kiss loved ones, stand still, and hold for several seconds. Tell them you missed them. Pets included.

▪ Then put on a high-energy song, dance, or move around.

▪ Go for a walk outside, any duration, alone, or with loved ones/dogs if able.

▪ List three items: what, who, and one thing about yourself that you are grateful for today.

CHECKLIST 6.2   STAYING CALM, AVOIDING ESCALATION, AND RETURNING TO SELF WHEN TRIGGERED

- Pay attention to your body. As soon as anger or discomfort arises, acknowledge it.
- Focus on NOT SPEAKING. The more uncomfortable you feel as you listen, and the more you want to speak, hold your tongue and stay silent.
- Take a slow deep breath through your nose with your mouth closed. Feel your chest wall expand in all dimensions; upward, outward, and downward as your diaphragm lowers, and then also anteriorly and posteriorly. Repeat.
- Pay attention to the situation as it unfolds. Stay silent. If another person is involved, at some point, there will be a pause and even awkward silence as your reaction is expected.
- Decide what to say to avoid escalation, no matter how much you disagree with or become upset by what you have heard. The more you disagree with the other's perspective, the more the discomfort and urge to reply with your perspective to show why they are "wrong".
- Consider asking the other person at least one or more questions about "WHY" he/she/they just shared what they shared. Most conversations and spoken words require more for us to understand the thought process, values, history, and intent or unintentional comment with impact.
- In clinical settings, whenever you find yourself in an interaction with any colleague, patient, supervisor, administrator, patient's family, etc., that creates discomfort, go to the top of this list and follow each step.
- Practice not feeling the need to "resolve" a situation at the moment unless it's patient safety related. Any conversation may be left peacefully with you verbalizing that you will take some time to consider what they said and you can resume the conversation another time.
- Being blindsided at any meeting is a highly triggering event, such includes not being informed by the person setting up the meeting with you what the meeting or conversation is about, or a meeting to discuss your performance. The latter will trigger much defensiveness which is expected.
- Express the need to take a moment and for space. Walk away for 2–3 minutes. Breathe and nothing else. Activate your parasympathetics first and always, without action.

■ Practice de-escalation using "mirroring", a natural human behavior describing when a person subconsciously imitates the gesture, speech pattern, energy, or attitude of another, especially in social situations. Humans notice many nonverbal communication cues such as facial expression, body language, gentle touch, smile, or kindness in one's eyes.

■ Listen for mood and tone of voice. Our tone of speech follows thought. If we are defensive, angry, reactive, irritated, stressed, or threatened, our speech pattern and tone will convey such emotions and moods. The moods and emotions of those who experience us in our emotional state are likely to mirror ours, and vice versa.

■ Practice pre-determined short sentences to say to yourself for times of stress and reactive state to self-soothe. Self-soothing activities include playing musical instruments, listening to your favorite music, nature sounds, brief or long meditations, walking outside, exercising, journaling, and/or visual imagery and listening to soothing sounds.

■ Ask yourself, why are you feeling how you feel? Acknowledge the emotions, let them be, and know that they will pass. As good as you think the other deserves and should lash out, don't.

CHECKLIST 6.3   ROUTINES TO INCREASE SENSE OF CONTROL OUTSIDE OF WORK

■ Journal. Write a sentence, paragraph, or full page. Whatever comes to mind. Start by recalling any event, emotions will follow.

■ Listen to the "Daily Calm" on Calm APP or any daily affirmation on another App.

■ When you see a flower, in your yard or anywhere, smell and inhale deeply.

■ Find a spot, any spot, and sit still for 5 minutes without a phone or any device.

■ Make a cup of tea or coffee, sit, and sip slowly.

■ Call, not text, a loved one, a friend, or someone you haven't spoken to in a while.

■ Focus on a single health choice you made today, food, activity, or decision that was great for your physical, emotional, or psychological wellbeing.

- Write a THANK YOU card, or any card, knowing they will be glad to receive it.
- Cook a great meal, no matter the time commitment or recipies you choose.
- As soon as you walk into the house after work, first, hug and kiss loved ones, hug for a few seconds, and stand still. Tell them you missed them. Pets included.
- Consider putting on a song, dance, or move around.
- Go for a walk outside, any duration, alone, or with loved ones/dogs if able.

CHECKLIST 6.4   POSSIBILITIES FOR OUTSOURCING FOR HOME/DOMESTIC LIFE

- Landscaper (unless therapeutic for you or your partner)
- Pool cleaning
- House cleaning (weekly, twice a month, or monthly depending on how messy, how many children, pets, and other factors)
- Handyman, electrician, plumber, indoor/outdoor pest control, appliance repair, snow removal, deck cleaning, etc.
- Part-time or full-time nanny(s) (especially for two physician households)
- Babysitter
- Tutoring for children as needed
- Eldercare
- Car washing and detailing
- Meal preparation
- Grocery shopping/delivery
- Dry cleaning (pick-up and delivery)
- Pay someone to organize and clean out your closet on an as-needed basis.
- Don't forget your family members, especially those whose own parents or in-laws are healthy, retired, and want to provide part-time or full-time help, intermittently, or as needed to provide childcare and/or driving to and from activities. Don't take them for granted, consider paying them in some way, financially or otherwise.
- Personal assistant to help manage family schedule and/or work schedule, cover miscellaneous tasks for children, family, pets, and whatever you need.

CHECKLIST 6.5   SUGGESTED ACTIVITIES FOR EXPERIENCING WELLBEING

- Monthly, bi-monthly massage therapy (weekly or as often as possible for surgeons: neck, shoulder, back)
- Counseling (individual and/or couples therapy)
- Manicure/pedicure (variable depending on individual preference)
- Workout/exercise classes (yoga, tennis, Pilates, pickle ball, spin, tai-chi, etc.)
- Walking dates with children, spouse, partner, any friend(s), and/or neighbor(s)
- Take a class or lessons (kickboxing, dancing, art, golf, piano, singing, guitar, cooking)
- Scheduled "date nights" for self/partner.
- Frequent meals with friends and new relationships you want to grow.
- Invite friends over for game night, or family game night.
- Once a month host dinner for others; someone who lives alone, or one or two couples or more, or new people you want to get to know better. If including children, get a sitter at your house.
- If you ± your partner walk your dog, invite another with a friendly dog to join.
- Playdates for children (home, parks, outdoors, public library)
- Schedule time to read, pick a favorite book or two, and indulge with a cup of tea/snack.
- An intentional list of movies and shows to indulge in while folding laundry or doing mindless tasks.
- When walking outdoors, always look to capture at least 3–4 photos of nature, flowers, or something beautiful.
- Close your eyes when outdoors and try to discern how many different birds you hear singing.
- Spend a couple of hours at a bookstore, grab a coffee/drink, read magazines, or browse books.
- Plan a vacation; look up images and information (use ChatGPT to help you) about the destination, find great restaurants, read reviews, and make a list of top sights and activities.
- If the above doesn't relax you, ask a friend/colleague for their past itinerary to save money on a travel agent.
- If you don't know people who travel and can provide itineraries, and don't enjoy planning, then find the best travel agent and provide enough details so your trip is planned well in advance.

- Look ahead six months, and before the start of every academic year, review your personal and professional calendars. For those with children, get the school calendar as soon as possible for the academic year. Review all dates kids are out of school and submit vacation dates accordingly so as to maximize long weekends when not on call and plan travel.
- Schedule time to hand write cards, or send letters instead of texts, to loved ones and those that matter the most to you, even if your handwriting is not pretty or legible.

Chapter 7

Financial Checklist

There are many factors that can make physicians particularly financially vulnerable over the course of their careers. For instance, medical, dental, and other healthcare professional degrees graduate with some of the highest debt-to-income ratios in the US.[1–3] For all of the sacrifices they had to make to get through medical school, residency, and fellowship training, often after incurring massive debt, the transition from training to an "attending" status may lead to poor financial decisions including overindulgence and excessive spending the moment they transition to a higher salary. That can put many physicians in even deeper financial stress.

It is beyond the scope of this book and chapter, or intent, to discuss how to achieve wealth, financial success or get the most out of one's medical and surgical career from a financial perspective. I consider myself lucky to have been a first-generation immigrant, with parents who were excellent in modeling responsible behavior when it comes to financial decision making. There are so many factors that influence how any individual "*feels*" about money.

Everyone has variable beliefs, thoughts, emotional attachment, spending and saving habits, ability and commitment to practice deferred gratification, manage expenses, and willingness to focus on debt management. The risks to physicians lie in the fact that as professional doctors are considered high-earners, and perceive themselves as such, they often make spending decisions knowing they enjoy stable income and employment status. What really matters is not how much a physician or anyone makes, but how quickly and how much they spend against their earnings.

A friend and financial expert who works with professional athletes once told me that he has observed often how professionals live with false financial security based on their annual salary without realizing how much they spend. An athlete who makes 2 million dollars per year, but spends 4 million per year, acquires debit rather quickly. Similarly, a physician may be lured by a six-digit sign-on bonus, with an expected annual salary ranging between $225,000 and $350,000 or more as they start their career. Upon making one's first annual salary, if expenses are drastically increased due to mortgage on a larger than necessary or extravagant house, high-end vehicle(s), clothing, jewelry, travel, extravagant meals, and miscellaneous "splurge" spending, without clear financial plan or understanding of total expenditure, a physician may easily acquire greater credit card debt on top of existing debt from years of training at far lower income. Meanwhile, credit card debts will increase exponentially as interest accrues at high rates.

I am so lucky that my husband happens to be incredibly logical, appropriately frugal, yet always supportive of my spending more on quality clothing, what fits and makes me feel great, for work and especially professional meetings and social engagements. The most constructive habit we have shared in 20 years of marriage, is that we discuss any large purchase with one another and decide based on our current checking and money market account balances as well as impending expenses which may not have been planned for. Air conditioners need repair or replacement, leaks occur, rodents may be found in one's attic, and several unpredictable yet necessary expenses related to house and car ownership or other miscellaneous "stuff" may happen. Far more stressful yet necessary, are unanticipated health issues resulting in medical expenses. While Dave and I may not always agree on what to buy, when to buy, or if we buy something at all, I am grateful we discuss our perspectives and come to a consensus. We decided long ago that he would handle all the bills, as I have anxiety and worry about our expenses and whether we have saved enough. Every person and couples in relationships deals with money differently, and may even have different accounts and bill pay structures and routines. The following checklist is aimed at creating financial protection and safety, for any physician but particularly trainees before they start their first job.

CHECKLIST 7.1 ACTIONS TO TAKE DURING OR IMMEDIATELY AFTER TRAINING

- Find a great financial advisor (experienced and physician-centric) if don't already have one.
- Discuss with FA, and confirm monthly automatic savings (20% at least) that are set up as AUTO Draft from a checking account to a money market account ("rainy day" cash reserve fund).

- Review total debt, interest rates, and exact monthly payments.
- Review your loan repayment terms, which are private vs public, public loans can extend payments. Set up AUTO DRAFTS for monthly minimal payment once exhaust all deferrals. Confirm the timeline to achieve interest rate reduction by making on-time payments every month.
- Explore all options for loan forgiveness.
- Discuss with FA and ask FA to help you enroll in employer benefits, especially retirement benefits and investment options. Some have waiting periods. Always MAXIMIZE contributions when able and know how much the employer is matching.
- Ask FA to help complete group benefit enrollment.
- If starting a solo practice, ask about SEP, SIMPLE IRA, Solo 401k, IRA, or ROTH IRA
- Ask FA to set up both IRA and Roth IRA as soon as you have taxable income.
- Discuss the best strategy and creation of a financial action plan based on marital status: single, married, divorced, engaged, with or without dependents, single or dual-income household. A great FA will outline and review all sources of income, current assets, anticipated recurrent monthly and large intermittent expenses, and most importantly advise steps to start and create an investment portfolio. Additionally, FA should ensure savings and investments are aligned with values, needs, wants, and longer-term protection against unanticipated events.
- Get a disability insurance policy if you don't already have one. If you do, increase DI coverage to reflect new income (must be True Own Occupation coverage). Best to do this BEFORE finishing training to receive discounted rates.
- Work with FA to establish life insurance, "Human Value Life" – suggest 15× income. There can be more than one type, variable, and term life insurance.
- Purchase umbrella liability coverage, at least $1–$3 million. Reach out to your homeowners/auto insurance agent to discuss cost, anticipate $400–$600 per year.
- Have an attorney review and update your will if you had one from another state. Also, have an attorney to draft Advance Directives, and set up Trusts, and American depository receipts (ADRs).

- If you have a business or LLC, have an attorney review the business structure and updates needed if moving to a state different than where the business was set up.
- Review state laws for your new state of residence for asset protection, malpractice, tort reform, liability, etc.

CHECKLIST 7.2 ACCOUNTS AND PLANS PHYSICIANS SHOULD KNOW ABOUT

- **403(b) plan**: Retirement account for tax-exempt organizations (hospitals which are non-profit), or government employees, school administrators, nurses, doctors, teachers, professors, etc.
- **Traditional 403(b)**: Allows one to have pretax money automatically deducted from each paycheck and paid/transferred into a personal retirement account. The advantage is that this reduces a physician's gross income and taxes will be deferred and due on when the employee withdraws it. Money taken out before age 59 ½ is subject to a 10% tax penalty with few exceptions such as becoming disabled, needing to pay for qualified medical expenses, and/or separating from the employer at age 55 or older.
- **Roth 403(b)**: Requires using after-tax dollars to go into the account. While now there is no immediate tax advantage, employees will not owe any more taxes on this saved money or profit it accrues when it is withdrawn.
- **401(k) plan**: A retirement savings plan that is company sponsored, with tax advantage for the employer. The employer agrees to pay a percentage of each paycheck directly to the investment account, and then match part or all that contribution. The employer is the one who chooses investment options including mutual funds.
- **401(k)** can also be traditional or Roth.
- **Individual Retirement Account (IRA)**: Personal retirement savings account that allows any individual to contribute up to a certain amount annually with tax advantages like 401(k).
- **529 plan**: A tax-advantaged college savings plan that is state-sponsored and an investment plan which allows one to save money for a beneficiary, usually a child, and use the money including the growth of the fund for future education expenses including tuition, books, by

a state or state agency. Originally limited to postsecondary education costs, it's been expanded to cover K-12 education in 2017 and apprenticeship programs in 2019. Now after the "SECURE Act" (Setting Every Community Up for Retirement Enhancement Act, 2020), 529s can also be used to pay off student loans and fund a Roth IRA.

■ There are two types of 529 plans: *educational savings plans* and *prepaid tuition plans*.

■ **Simplified Employee Pension (SEP) Plan**: Retirement plan for self-employed individuals and small business owners that allow contributions to a tax-deferred investment account.

■ **Profit Sharing Plan**: An employer-sponsored retirement plan that allows employers to make contributions to an investment account on behalf of their employees, based on the company's profits.

■ **Health Savings Plan (HSA)**: A tax-advantaged savings account that one can use to pay for qualified medical expenses and available to those with a high-deductible health plan (HDHP). HDHP usually has lower monthly premiums. Money in HSA can be invested and grow tax-free, and withdrawals for qualified medical expenses are also tax-free such as when used for doctor's visits, prescription medications, and medical procedures. HSA balance rolls over from year to year so one can save unused funds for future expenses. Since not all medical expenses are eligible for HSA reimbursement, it's important to discuss with your FA and tax professional/accountant to understand the rules and regulations better.

Disability Benefits

Make sure you have an "own occupation disability insurance policy", which covers individuals who become disabled and are unable to perform most of the occupational duties that they have been trained to perform. This means that if you can't do your job, you will be paid this benefit even if you work doing other jobs but they are not the occupational duties that you were trained for. For example, had my disability been permanent and I couldn't work as a surgeon, but started working in non-ENT, non-surgeon type work, my policy and benefits would continue despite income from other types of work. Benefits are reduced gradually once they exceed 20% of your pre-disability earnings and stop at 85% of pre-disability earnings for the initial policy and 80% for the second policy. So, if you made $500,000 pre-disability, you could make $100k doing another job of your choosing and collect full benefits. Between $100,000 and $400,000 for Policy

2 and $100,000 and $425,000 for Policy 1, the benefits are gradually reduced. I've attached some definitions below.

Regular Occupation: Your occupation at the time Disability begins. If You have limited Your practice to a professionally recognized specialty in medicine or law, the specialty will be deemed to be Your Regular Occupation. If You are retired at the time Disability begins, being retired will be deemed to be Your Regular Occupation.

Residual Disability/Residually Disabled: Residual Disability means you are not totally disabled, but because of your injury or sickness:

1. Your monthly earnings are reduced by 20% or more of your indexed prior monthly earnings; and
2. You are under the regular care of a physician appropriate for your injury or sickness.

    and

3. You are able to:
    a. Do some, but not all, of the substantial and material duties of your regular occupation; or
    b. Do all of the substantial and material duties of your regular occupation, but not for as long a time or as effectively as you did immediately prior to your injury or sickness.

Chapter 8

Physical and Mental Health Checklist

Physician's Own Health: We Must Treat Ourselves as Patient #1

Physicians are well versed in informing their patients and others about the critical importance of regular exercise, staying physically active, eating a healthy and balanced diet, avoiding excessive sugar-sweetened beverages (SSBs) like soda, stopping smoking, limiting alcohol, wearing seat belts, and making lifestyle changes if one is found to have less than "healthy" status based on labs, tests, and symptoms. Yet many physicians do not apply the same counseling nor commit to change for themselves. Why? I can't speak for all physicians, but as a chronically exhausted surgeon, committed to excelling in clinical care, research, leadership roles, and teaching, without compromising my own family's wellbeing and my constant effort to cook, clean, feed, schedule, and command much logistics of our home life, I spent years simply telling myself I didn't have any "TIME". Who has time to wake up early and exercise when I already leave the house at 6:30 am? And who has time to exercise when I get home hungry and rush to get dinner on the table before 7 pm?

I sure didn't believe it was possible, and while as a family we walked, I played weekend tennis, I always believed routine exercise was available only to women who didn't work, or people who were simply "built" differently. After meeting Dr. Jim Loehr, a world-renowned sports psychologist whose clients included world-renowned tennis players like Pete Sampras and Andre Agassi, and taking

DOI: 10.4324/9781003452478-9

his Johnson and Johnson Human Performance Institute for Energy Management Training and subsequently becoming a certified trainer for that program, did I realize my excuses and consequences of not taking accountability. I lived those consequences for the past two years as I struggled against medical disability, frozen shoulder, cervical radiculopathy from years of poor surgical ergonomics, never stretching, lacking core and muscle strength, and simply never treating my body as a worn-out machine that did not have regular tune-ups as the miles far exceeded ideal maintenance targets over the past few decades. My body was not one I could upgrade, trade-in, or give up for a new model. Injury, disability, severe pain, and terminal diagnoses can all help a physician and especially surgeons accept a simple reality: we too are human.

The culture and system created the most unfortunate and deeply ingrained belief that we simply CAN'T take a break, stop, call out sick when feeling ill, nor ever really consider what our bodies and minds really want when so many others are waiting for us, every day. Whether it's clinic appointments or surgeries, patients have waited, waited, and waited, to get that appointment and surgery date. If I call out, 25, 30, or more patients will be canceled, they will be so mad, disappointed, and what if something terrible happens to them because I wasn't there to do my job? Worse, canceled surgeries mean so many have already taken time out of their work schedule, arranged for loved ones to take time out, and even traveled from afar, to provide post-operative care. What is most anxiety-provoking really, is WHEN will we be able to reschedule ALL THESE PATIENTS to another day for clinics or surgeries? Of course, now I understand why it was so much easier to just get up, limp if needed, and go to work. By suffering, quietly or out loud, but if I do what's expected of me and the schedule already planned for me, weeks, and months in advance, suffering of one is always better than suffering for so many others.

How ridiculous, how horrible, and how sad. These past two decades of rarely calling out, unless I physically can't stand due to severe flu, or being hospitalized or in the emergency room for my abdominal "migraine" like pains, dehydration, bloody UTIs, and acute chest pain, I didn't know HOW to just give my body what it screamed to me that it needed. Turned out so many of these symptoms were warning signs, like unexplained hives for 30 days feeling like I was a witch being burned at a stake, angioedema waking me at 2 am as my face and lips were severely distorted and I feared for my airway as an ENT surgeon, and countless hours of chest pain, none of which were diagnosed by any Emergency Room doctors or specialist with clear diagnoses. My body was warning me that it was shutting down. Repeatedly and over time, my body screamed louder and louder because I simply ignored and disconnected my visceral feelings from my mind.

I have lost several dear friends, best friends, colleagues, and co-workers to cancer of various types, always unexpected, some at a very young age, leaving spouses and children behind, and some as recently as two years ago. What I have learned from sharing in their struggles and journey when forced to navigate their own healthcare, as well as from supporting those who struggle now against medical illnesses, have taught and inspired me to continue sharing with others WHY physicians need to focus on their own health and be accountable for themselves to ensure their longevity and wellbeing for the sake of their loved ones and those who depend on them. What I didn't think possible happened, I am now in a routine of going to the gym, walking, ensuring I stretch my shoulders, focusing on my posture, identifying any pain and addressing it, and taking time away from a highly intense, unrelenting, overly scheduled career allowed me to live with awareness that I would never have gained. My body trusts me a little more now than ever before. I know now that I was not the chosen one to save the world. Ensuring I live with optimal wellbeing is the only way I can ensure my ability to support the wellbeing of others, patients, or anyone I care for.

As I am not a psychologist, psychiatrist, or licensed mental health counselor, this chapter was written from the perspective of, first, a human who has suffered bouts of depression due to early parental loss, relationship challenges, and most importantly traumatic events through my career as a surgeon. The checklists below are written based on personal and professional experiences over the past two decades having been supported intermittently by incredible counselors.

Additionally, personal reflections during, after, and well after events, along with intentional self-directed learning on how one heals, have inspired me to share some suggestions on where and *HOW*, to find a dedicated psychologist or counselor, especially for busy physicians and surgeons. Various books, lectures, and meetings with authors and fellow physicians who have shared their wisdom through personal experiences, have all contributed to my ever-evolving perspective on *FEELING* "*well*" rather than "unwell". I have created a network of mental health counselors who I am able to quickly connect to physicians in need.

CHECKLIST 8.1   CHECKLIST FOR OPTIMAL PHYSICAL WELLBEING

- Find a great primary care physician.
- Schedule routine annual checkups with labs and additional labs based on age, symptoms, concerns, and biologic changes including perimenopausal or menopausal phase of life for females.
- Schedule dental cleaning every six months, and acute dental care as needed.
- All preventive and diagnostic care, mammogram, EGD, pap smear, colonoscopy, etc.

- See a physical therapist or occupational therapist (OT) for any current or physical limitations or symptoms, pain, or decreased range of motion, and get a formal assessment.
- Make appointments with highly recommended subspecialists as needed.
- Routine exercise at least three times per week, including both cardio and weight bearing. Doesn't matter what but must be what you love.
- Cut out the sodas, excessively sweetened juices, coffee drinks that are high in sugar, energy drinks, and anything that's not water.
- Water, more water, more water.
- No tobacco. None. If need motivation, search videos on head and neck cancer resections, and tracheostomy dependency.
- Check vitamin D level for possible deficiency, then take supplementation as needed.
- Wear sunscreen and sunblock.
- Sleep; protect sleep instead of chronic late-night binge-watching of TV or internet use.
- Avoid processed foods if you can't identify all ingredients, ensure when it was made, or can't pronounce all the ingredients easily.
- When grocery shopping, ensure most of the cart is beautifully colored with fresh fruits and vegetables, and learn to cook uncomplicated meals that are not time-consuming but high in fiber and nutrient-packed.
- Floss slowly and carefully, daily.
- For female physicians, learn about pelvic floor health. Even if you have never had children, pelvic floor health is something no one talks about yet a critical component of women's health especially with age and with onset and after menopause.
- Never underestimate the power of a hot or cold shower, or a nice bath after every workday.
- Practice slow and deep breathing. Sit or stand up tall and straight. Feel the entire chest wall expanding with inspiration against your closed mouth and count slowly. Repeat
- Snack strategically, and avoid hypoglycemia by ensuring you don't go more than 2–3 hours without a 100–150 calorie snack. Great options include nuts, edamame, whole fruit, high-protein low-sugar options, and avoid donuts and sugary snacks. (intermittent need for chocolate is fully expected, and requires no justification)

- Given physicians can't be trusted to be objective about their own health and willingness to seek or ask for help, identify a "buddy" fellow physician and make a pact that will help you ensure others seek help and get to appointments in a timely fashion.
- Try hiking, either trails around you or plan parts of your vacations and trips by looking up nearby trails and then enjoying a beautiful enhanced "walk" in nature. A great app is AllTrails (https://www.alltrails.com/) which will find and provide details, photos, locations, and reviews of trails anywhere!
- Stop eating and drinking alcohol or SSBs, except water, for 2 hours before bedtime. This reduces physiologic reflux which will make you feel "bloated", sluggish, tired, have heartburn/indigestion and increase the risk of snoring, poor sleep, or need to wake at night to go to the bathroom and urinate.
- Avoid excessive sugar, alcohol, dairy, heavy meals, high caloric meals, fried foods, and foods that prolong gastric emptying time. (for more information, go to www.ahealthierwei.com, or simply review ASA NPO guidelines created based on gastric emptying time).
- Consider using humidifier in bedroom. Even if you have air conditioning on in your home daily, using a simple humidifier will improve nasal hygiene, breathing, decrease congestion and stuffy nose, which increase mouth breathing and decrease quality of sleep.
- Be sure that at night, your bedroom temperature is on cooler side. For optimal sleep, recommended temperature is between 60°F and 68°F. To save money, our AC is set at 72°F. Everyone may vary but the cooler, the better.

CHECKLIST 8.2   CHECKLIST FOR OPTIMAL MENTAL WELLBEING

- Find an incredible psychologist, psychiatrist, or mental health counselor. Consider looking for someone with experience specifically working with physicians/surgeons.
- Schedule a session with the counselor/psychologist/psychiatrist. Your professional and/or personal life does not need to be "broken" for you to create time and space and listen to yourself describe your current mental health.

- Consider finding career, litigation, surgical, and/or other types of physician expert coaches or coaches who have expertise for working with physicians.
- Schedule routine exercise into your schedule for the sake of your mental health. Research has continued to validate and highlight how exercise, even in short spurts, or exercise "snacks", can reduce risk of chronic illness, boost mental health, and reduce depression and anxiety.
- Take a validated burnout survey, be honest and prepare to act if the "score" suggests you are in moderate to high degree of burnout. There are several surveys you can take.
- Have a great cry sometimes. Give yourself permission to express your emotions. Enjoy watching a tearjerker, or creating time alone and space to allow suppressed feelings and acknowledge your emotions to surface as visceral sensations.
- Listen and pay attention to your inner voice, visceral feelings, moods, and emotions. If you are easily irritable, angry, experience deep feelings of sadness, lethargy, lack interest to engage with others, please reach out to someone you trust, family, friends, or colleagues, but most of all, consider a professional counselor.
- Change your inner voices that judge you for how you "feel" and makes your own mental health and need for support a "weakness", "deficiency", not being "tough" enough, nor any narrative where you are judging yourself and somehow should "feel" differently.
- If you are a physician/surgeon who has experienced ANY or many of the following on the checklist below, please consider seek professional counseling.

CHECKLIST 8.3 EVENTS EXPERIENCED DESERVING OF COUNSELING TO INCREASE MENTAL WELLBEING

- Litigation
- Receiving threats from patients/patient families: physical, verbal, and/or via social media
- Unanticipated adverse events, sentinel events, and/or events resulting in permanent harm or death to a patient under your care or your team's care.
- Witnessing or participating in the care of a patient who experienced significant traumatic postop or care complications, excessive and

uncontrollable bleeding intraop, postop, or during any procedures and/or hospitalization.

- Witnessing or participating in unsuccessful resuscitations
- Bearing witness to and/or participating in the clinical care of patients who endured trauma, gun violence, sexual abuse, physical abuse, horrific unusual injuries, mutilation, and any or all iatrogenic injuries from other humans.
- Any of the above but in children and/or any vulnerable subpopulations, or someone with similar ethnicity, race, gender orientation, or characteristics like you
- Bearing witness to and/or supporting navigation of care of patients with injuries due to unusual, unhealthy, immoral, and/or human rights violations, involuntary suffering imposed by others.
- Traumatic injuries to children due to abuse
- Bearing witness to and/or participating in the care of patients who were harmed by tragedies that impact families such as multiple deaths from automobile accidents, natural disasters, mass gun violence, unanticipated accidents, and/or any unusual circumstances.
- Being a patient yourself, enduring any care-related complications, pain, delayed or misdiagnoses.

Survey Instruments to Measure Physician Burnout

Maslach Burnout Inventory (MBI): https://www.mindgarden.com/315-mbi-human-services-survey-medical-personnel

AMA Mini Z Survey: You can complete and submit to stepsforward@ama-assn.org who will follow up and provide your results to you.

Oldenburg Burnout Inventory: It can measure burnout in any occupation. A 16-item survey with positively and negatively framed items that covers two areas – exhaustion (physical, cognitive, and affective aspects) and disengagement from work.

Stanford Professional Fulfillment Index: A 16-item survey which measures burnout and professional fulfillment in physicians.

The Wellbeing Index: https://www.mywellbeingindex.org/

For more descriptions and how to access each survey, go to https://nam.edu/valid-reliable-survey-instruments-measure-burnout-well-work-related-dimensions/

CHECKLIST 8.4 HOW PHYSICAL EXERCISE/ACTIVITY IMPROVES MENTAL HEALTH

- You will feel proud, strong, and happy by taking accountability for your own body, mind, and wellbeing and live your best life.
- As you take action to feel and look better, instead of possible self-criticism because of your weight, or body appearance, and/or misalignment between what you think you should do but regret you haven't, or live with conflicting inner voices, taking action no matter how small or how large, will change your from being "victim" to being in charge and having a sense of control.
- Schedule a session with the counselor/psychologist/psychiatrist. Your professional and/or personal life does not need to be "broken" for you to create time and space and listen to yourself describe your current mental health.
- Stimulate and increase the release of endorphins or neurochemicals especially beta-endorphin and beta-lipotrophin, which are natural mood enhancers to help feel positive and happy while decreasing symptoms of depression and anxiety.
- Routine exercise and physical exertion or activities reduce stress and optimize stress management by reducing cortisol release, and/or help the body regulate cortisol levels.
- While exercising or being physically active, often one has relief from worrying thoughts, rumination, and anxiety, but instead focuses on the physical activities or performance.
- Opportunity to connect socially while achieving individual and collective benefits; walking with someone or in groups, cycling in groups, tennis, pickle ball, pilates, yoga, or any other classes where you can do what you enjoy with others.
- Opportunity to meet new people, with social and/or professional connections that can positively influence your "being".
- Having better physical health should support more energy, and physical abilities to enjoy activities in personal and professional lives without the frustrations, suffering, acute or chronic pain, and interruption from desired and optimal daily activities simply by needing less medical and/or surgical treatments.
- Physical activities that involve being outdoors provide exposure to sunlight, which is critical for regulating our circadian rhythm. The timing of physiological processes in our body depends on

photoreceptors in our eyes being exposed to light. Additionally, light exposure regulates our melatonin production. Sunlight exposure improves mood and increases energy levels by stimulating our bodies to produce serotonin which increases feelings of wellbeing and happiness. Finally, with optimal circadian rhythm, well-regulated sleep schedule, sleep hygiene, and achieving high-quality sleep, we experience better physical health and mental health.

- When was the last time you had a great sweat from physical activity and not just hot weather? Enjoy the great feeling in the shower after exercise or activity-induced sweating.
- The less you move, the less energy your body produces. The more you move, the more you will feel energetic and alive. Physical movement increases circulation, and as we increase respiratory rate, we also increase oxygen which through circulation results in cellular respiration. That means mitochondria cells will produce adenosine triphosphate (ATP) which is the energy currency for life.

Chapter 9

Relationship Checklist

Both personal and professional relationships require time, energy, intentional effort, and most importantly experiencing mutual trust between two people. Due to various factors and work environments that are highly stressful, inflexible schedules, and a career and professional culture that expects physicians to always prioritize everyone else except themselves, there are some unique challenges for physicians when it comes to creating nurturing and fulfilling relationships with themselves and then others.

This chapter's checklists will help readers nurture and protect their romantic and platonic relationships despite constant busyness and pressure. Example items on the checklist include finding a counselor and various suggestions for spontaneous or recurring scheduled activities to enhance connection and communication with partners, spouses, and loved ones. In addition, this chapter will also suggest an approach to building long-lasting and deeper friendships and relationships using a "who, when, and how" framework.

CHECKLIST 9.1   CHECKLIST TO HELP PHYSICIANS CONNECT DEEPLY WITH PARTNERS/SPOUSES

- Ensure scheduled times daily at home, and especially on weekends, to SIT and TALK with your partner or spouse. The best times are early mornings over coffee (5–10 mins), after arriving home (first change out of work clothes, can spend few minutes before arriving in

---

 DOI: 10.4324/9781003452478-10

the garage, while parked in the garage, or once inside to consciously remind oneself NOT to rehearse or relive the day's stress, frustrations, anger, or challenges to your spouse/partner), or after dinner.

■ Be aware that the bullet above is NOT the same as all other communications related to children, pets, anyone else regardless of family or friends, any conversation related to other people's needs, household logistics, SCHEDULES and appointments, responsibilities, actions required of the other partner, any timelines, deadlines, "to-do lists", "did you ____"? (pick up, take out, call, contact, remember to, go get, fix the____, etc.).

■ There will never be a shortage of functional and outcome-related communication required of any domestic and personal life demands. The shortage of the most critical and meaningful conversations are the ones that require one's FULL attention, creating space, not interrupting, or solving (as physicians do all day long in any healthcare setting), nor can be achieved while "multi-tasking".

■ Can sit in the bathroom while partner/spouse is showering, a great time to catch up about the day.

■ Create routines as a couple to maximize time together. This creates bonding. This creates bonding simply by you sharing in each other's awareness, space, consciousness, and routine which adds up to countless minutes and hours and feeling you are a "couple".

■ Take each other to the airport, when possible, (with or without the kids), even though you could take a rideshare. Pick each other up from the airport, even if you or your partner/spouse can take a rideshare.

■ Before going to sleep, can hold hands and pick something lighthearted to watch for a few minutes, or if you can't find anything you agree on or both enjoy, try YouTube travel guide Ryan Shirley's countless videos. He uses drones to film extraordinary calming videos of the most gorgeous places on earth, in various countries, and continents, and is a travel guide. These videos have soothing music and stunning imagery, and can be very calming. Furthermore, you and your partner can discuss if you would consider planning travel to such locations that interest you.

■ Walk together and with a dog if you have one. Early mornings are the best, if not during the week, then at least one morning on weekends. Listen to birdsongs and notice tree leaves, flowers, neighborhoods, or nature if you find a local trail. Do not talk about logistics, instead, ask each other how he/she/they are feeling and how the past day or week has been. Most importantly, how do they "feel" and what would help them feel "better".

- When physically apart, send flowers or a small token of appreciation to your spouse/partner if you are the one traveling for medical/surgical conferences or any professional meetings. Send a note that expresses gratitude to your partner/spouse for taking care of the children/home and giving you the opportunity to travel, participate, and spend time with colleagues for personal and professional development.
- Find a great couples or marriage counselor. Counseling is not just for when couples are reaching the brink of separation and/or divorce. In fact, having some early in the marriage helps you understand each other's family history, past relationship issues with self and others, as well as understand what the specific triggers are and WHY, for everyone.
- Early counseling allows a third-party to help you and your spouse/partner agree on rules of engagement, and impact on the other based on the communication and behavior style of the partner/spouse.
- Most humans, particularly physicians, are never taught how to ask for what he/she/they need or want. Practice asking for what you need and want. It can be as simple as being held, being complimented, being listened to generously, being seen and heard without any words or actions. Physicians are masters at suppressing. They suppress their reactions, judgment, thoughts, fear, uncertainty, anger, and even sadness every day as it's required and crucial to effectively care for patients and make constant decisions. Similarly, similar withholding from colleagues and work partners may also occur, creating conflict and even resentment.
- Find, create, and make time for shared hobbies. If that doesn't happen, find activities that both can agree to do at least.
- Share sunrise and/or sunsets, as many as possible, as often as possible. You will feel more connected EVERY TIME. Does not require fancy vacations or exotic travel to achieve this. Find spots in your neighborhood, city, and/or locations near you.
- Encourage one another to seek counseling to support mental health, situational or otherwise. As a spouse and partner, one can't "fix" or address challenges we all face with our own past trauma and pain, and can benefit from professional counseling to create a more positive

narrative and healthy relationship with ourselves before we can contribute our best selves to others.

- Tell each other jokes, not one, but many. Nothing like deep belly laughs, the kind that brings tears out, and increase the risk of momentary incontinence, or accidental farting, which reflect the heartfelt joy and happiness.
- Share a beverage and snacks together, at random times, on weekends, just call a "timeout" during busy days or especially on vacation, to simply ENJOY each other's presence.
- Daily "Wordle" with spouse/partner/children/families/friends, when you share results, you are connecting with others.
- Always acknowledge and respect his/her/their emotions/moods/reactions in the moment. Do not respond to avoid escalation but simply BE. Allow time and space for the other person to fully express what needs to come out. Wait. Wait until the other person is ready to re-engage. This is hard to do, takes so much practice. It's NOT always about you.

Chapter 10

Checklist for Career Longevity

I care deeply about protecting my own career longevity and that of all fellow physicians. This is not to say that I believe every physician should spend decades until their retirement practicing 100% clinical medicine and nothing else. In fact, I have embraced learning other ways to create income using my knowledge, education, and experiences that do not involve direct patient care.

What I have learned about the concept of career "longevity" is that much like life, those who want to live as long as possible, as healthy as possible, must practice discipline over their diet, exercise, sleep, and actions to achieve this goal. While for some physicians, it may be energizing, exhilarating, and liberating to shift from full-time clinical work to part-time, or shift their career to one outside of traditional direct patient care, the majority of American physicians likely want to continue practicing full-time until retirement. Strategies to ensure a healthy long career should be created instead of simply praying for health and the absence of tragic accidents and hoping the years go by quickly toward retirement as burn-out continues.

Why have doctors not been routinely offered a sabbatical when other industries and employees can enjoy such a benefit after a certain number of years at work? Even in traditional academic centers after achieving "tenured" associate or professor ranks, there is no one reminding or even facilitating physicians to plan and take their "sabbatical" as an intentional "time-out" to refresh and refocus one's purpose and future.

DOI: 10.4324/9781003452478-11

Sabbatical leave is an extended period away from work, granted to an employee for a variety of purposes, whether for personal or professional academic growth, learning a new skill, or simply rest and "recuperation", while being paid and maintaining their status with their employer. Physicians are not informed of this benefit, even opportunity, and hence when informed may not give themselves permission to take a leave of absence or break, to rejuvenate. Instead, they will work without strategic recovery, short or long, big or small, effective or not, until injury, the highest degree of burnout, or illness, and then make a drastic decision to leave or change jobs and practice. This checklist will cover self-compassion, self-trust, and critical use of self-reflection to live the life you intend to live, instead of one where you are always too busy, "drowning", and have come to believe you have no control or even a victim by pursuing this noble profession. You are responsible and capable of HOW you live, WHO you work for and with, and what you want your life and legacy to be. Finally, we owe it to ourselves to at least master our thoughts and exert control where we can over our bodies, minds, and lives, at work and outside of work.

CHECKLIST 10.1   CONSIDERATIONS TO ENSURE AND ENJOY CAREER LONGEVITY

- Follow prior checklists to optimize physical, mental, and professional wellbeing and safety. Career longevity is not possible without strong physical and mental health, as well as creating an incredible network of professionals to support you.
- If you work for, at, or have a faculty appointment with any academic institution, find out and ask about the institution's paid sabbatical leave policy. Then plan one if you qualify or even if not yet, make plans until you qualify for one.
- If you are not practicing in academic settings, but are employed by hospitals, health systems, private equity, national employer groups, multispecialty groups, or by whomever, figure out the best way to plan 4–6 weeks off in the near future or within the next year. You don't need a terminal diagnosis, nor your loved ones to get one, nor to be injured severely, to take planned time off.
- Consider joining a medical mission trip. Travel, work, and exposure to other cultures, populations, and their challenges in access to basic and expertise in subspecialty care, especially surgical, will inspire gratitude and appreciation for your reality.

- Identify aspects and components of your clinical practice that you love, then identify or enhance more activities in those areas; examples include working with a subpopulation of patients or clinical disease entities that is your grown expertise, clinical research, teaching, developing educational content, speaking, writing, and alternative media platform for disseminating educational content, podcasts, involvement with regional or national societies, taskforce, editorial review boards, advisor to local, regional, and national patient support groups for specific populations and diseases, volunteering as physician for youth sports camps, and creating/connecting physicians with similar interest in a group.
- Make time for honest reflection about whether you are content with your current work environment, the culture at your workplace, and the people that you work with. If you are happy, content, and grateful, as is your family, then express gratitude and contribute to such a work environment and the people who make that possible for you.
- If you are unhappy, frustrated, angry, dissatisfied, or often think of changing your job and work environment, LISTEN to your inner voice and plan for change. It is critical to understand exactly what, who, why, how, and all factors and reasons that have led you to such a state. Is there a lack of value alignment with your employer? Is the culture toxic? Just how many promises have not been kept? Is your leadership journey and/or professional development wasting away and unable to flourish due to lack of resources and/or support? Are you simply showing up daily to pay the bills and make a living? Or are you able to grow professionally and even thrive despite the challenges faced by most physicians?
- Take a break from some and decline some other professional and extracurricular activities if you have over-committed or know that you have outspent your time-to-fulfillment ratio. You can already return to the ones you care deeply about after regaining some space and time.
- Apply, interview, and seriously consider with your partner/spouse the possibility of change. New jobs, new cities, new opportunities, and new challenges often include the chance to try new leadership roles, increase in salary (you are always worth more to those you don't currently work for), responsibilities, or change to grow a practice or program.

- Branch out and explore options for passive and/or supplemental income, part-time consulting work, either in healthcare and your area of clinical expertise, or something entirely different. More and more physicians are investing in rental properties, creating alternative income streams, opening their own businesses including med spa, as advisors for startups in healthcare technology and other industries, etc.
- Ask yourself, what is the most "FUN" activity you have recently engaged in related to your work and job? Why was it fun for you? What did you love about that? Can you do more of it and get paid?
- Have a plan with adjusted clinical workload as you age, mature in your career, and as your life changes. Some know when they want to retire, or at least cut back from 100% clinical practice. Consider what would allow you to not leave your job and career prematurely, i.e., by decreasing to 80%, then 70 or 75%, or 50%, over time, and figure out what to do with the space you created. Most physicians truly enjoy interactions with patients.
- When or if you retire, or if working far less than you do now, consider serving as volunteer faculty for your local medical school. They often need clinicians to help teach first- and second-year students how to perform excellent history taking, physical exams, anatomy dissections, and/or serve as a mentor for research. Working with young energetic medical students is inspiring and eye-opening.
- Volunteer work at local free clinics, community health centers, and other organizations.
- Medical writing for the public or medical communities.
- Shift to activities that can incorporate medicine with art, music, writing, poetry, and any other activities you love.

For many clinicians, staying in one institution/hospital can be the pathway to senior or executive leadership roles. As a woman, I have found the need to move when I hit a "ceiling" despite my efforts and accomplishments. There are too many factors outside one's control, including politics at the workplace, whom you report to, whether you have a strong sponsor and mentor at your current workplace, and if there is a strong and healthy culture between physician and non-physician executives in C-suite leadership at your hospital/system. Oftentimes, a health system's workplace culture, priorities, transparency, and how employees experience being "valued" including physicians, are positive or negative depending on who is in charge. For those in private practice settings, factors include senior partners and how they make decisions for the group, when they plan to retire, unanticipated management changes in the practice, financial stability and debt, contractual relationships with hospitals and/or insurance, and other personal and professional life challenges may require a planned or unplanned change in employment and location of the practice.

Chapter 11

Checklists for Ergonomics, Disability, and Recovery

Until my own disability and realizing the anatomical and functional issues I experienced from developing a frozen shoulder, and how my degenerative cervical spine caused numbness and tingling of my right hand and fingers, I had not heard of nor knew anything about ergonomics as a science and its relevance to surgeons.

Ergonomics is a scientific discipline on the study of human factors, with a focus on understanding how we as humans interact with all other elements of a system or our environment. The study of ergonomics applies theory, principles, data, and methods to design what surrounds us to optimize our wellbeing and our overall performance in that "system".

There are three types of ergonomics: physical, cognitive, and organizational, with five specific aspects of ergonomics defined as safety, comfort, ease of use, productivity/performance, and aesthetics. The Center for Disease Control (CDC) defines ergonomics as the scientific study of people at work with the goal of preventing soft tissue injuries and what I have mentioned as work-related musculoskeletal disorders (WRMSD) which are caused by sudden or prolonged exposure to external force, vibrations, repetitive motion, and awkward posture and positioning that increase our risk of developing WRMSD.[1]

DOI: 10.4324/9781003452478-12

Last year, I had the great fortune of being introduced to Dr. Geeta Lal (highlighted in Chapter 5), a now dear friend who is a coach specifically for surgical ergonomics, and current president of the Society of Surgical Ergonomics which I joined proudly as a member last year. This society has a mission to facilitate scientific dialogue, education, and innovation related to surgical ergonomics in the form of annual meetings, lectures, circulation of scientific literature, and research. For any reader, especially surgeons, anesthesiologists, and proceduralists, check out the society and consider joining. https://www.societyofsurgicalergonomics.org/

While I am not an expert on surgical or physical ergonomics, I have learned much from leaders in the industry about wearable technology for physicians for optimal wellbeing, I have created this checklist below for surgeons and those who perform repetitive motions in surgery or any procedures including colonoscopy, interventional radiology procedures, bronchoscopies, esophagogastroduodenoscopies (EGDs), and others.

CHECKLIST 11.1 CHECKLIST FOR OPTIMAL PHYSICAL AND SURGICAL ERGONOMICS

- Avoid using and carrying any "briefcase" or shoulder bag on one side. Use roller bags if usually carrying charts, paperwork, and tons of "stuff" to and from work on a daily basis.
- Avoid looking down when using cell phone and texting. Minimize repeated and prolonged neck flexion position.
- Purchase and use the Upright GO 2 Premium Posture Corrector Trainer and Tracker with Smart App. https://www.uprightpose.com/
- For all surgeons, include "ergonomic check" during pre-incision WHO "TimeOut"
- Anti-Fatigue Mats
- SensorGel cold touch contour gel-infused memory foam pillow.
- Have the Operating Room (OR) table height adjusted based on the tallest person involved in the surgical case.
- Use ergonomic stools/chairs.
- Sit as much as possible for entire or portions of surgical procedures.
- Take frequent breaks throughout the case, based on visceral sensations of discomfort or pain.
- Before, during, and after the case, perform OR stretch[2]
- Ensure operating microscopes are ergonomically adjusted.
- Ensure operating loupes have optimal declination to maintain a neutral craniovertebral angle. Wear the lightest lead apron available, and for as minimal amount of time as necessary.

- Perform OR stretch and/or against the wall while waiting for induction, prep, or turnover.
- Practice deep breathing exercises, before, during, and after the case
- Take "microbreaks" throughout the procedure.[3]
- Practice squeezing shoulder blades together, externally rotating the shoulders.
- Post OR days, consider scheduled massage therapy with a focus on the neck and shoulders.
- Find an excellent chiropractor and consider adjustments as needed.
- Consider scheduled Pilates and stretching classes or exercises.
- Wear very comfortable shoes, including lightweight exercise running or cross-training shoes.
- Post visual data and intervention reminders in OR, clinics, and throughout hospital settings on WRMSD and how to stretch and optimize ergonomic positions.
- Have human factor experts walk through the hospital to ensure monitors and workstations are ergonomically optimized for workers, including keyboard, mouse, stool, and chair heights.
- When at the gym, perform exercises that strengthen core and back muscles, between shoulder blades (i.e., rhomboids). For example, rowing, band pull-part, cable seated-row, any weights pulled toward body and squeeze shoulder blades together. Most physicians especially surgeons have shoulder postures that are overly internally rotated, and weak core as most humans.
- Do stretching exercises that open shoulders and increase shoulder mobility, shoulder rolls, standing wall stretching, look up on internet and/or consult PT.
- Formal consult by OT/PT to assess core strength, and work on releasing tension in scalene and paracervical muscles to reduce tightness in neck and shoulder.

CHECKLIST 11.2 SIGNS OF CERVICAL RADICULOPATHY

- When trying to ride a bike, raising both arms to hold bike handrails, feeling numbness and tingling down arms and hands.
- Developing numbness, tingling, and/or pain in fingers, hands, or arms
- Intermittent cyanosis of fingertips, fingers, and hands

- MRI demonstrating degenerative disks in single or multiple levels, stenosis of cervical foramina, or reduced flow of cerebrospinal fluid through foramina.
- Sudden onset severe pain in neck and/or arms
- Weakness of upper extremity or extremities
- Positive Spurling Test (Maximal Cervical Compression Test and Foraminal Compression Test): performed by positioning the patient with neck extended and head rotated, then applying downward pressure on the head. The test is positive if the maneuver causes pain to radiate from the neck, shoulder, or arm in the same direction that the head is pointing, weakness in the neck muscles, tingling, numbness, or the sensation of pins and needles in the neck, shoulders, or arms. Altered tendon reflexes are also a sign of a positive test.
- Positive Hoffman Test and Hoffman's Sign: One holds out one's arms and open palm facedown, extending fingers in front of the person. The doctor flicks the middle fingernail, also known as the digital or snapping reflex, or Tromner's or Jakobsen's sign. If the thumb or forefinger moves after the flick, the Hoffman sign is positive which may indicate damage or abnormality to the upper region of the cervical spinal cord including compression.

CHECKLIST 11.3 SIGNS OF CARPEL TUNNEL SYNDROME

- Numbness and tingling when trying to ride a bike, with both hands on handrails, a feeling of numbness and tingling down arms and hands.
- Numbness and tingling in hands and fingers in thumb, index finger, middle finger, or ring finger.
- Electric shock or "lightening" sensation in hands and fingers.
- Pain – intermittent or constant, in the wrist, hand, and/or forearm. Pain may be worse at night.
- Develop weakness in hands which impacts the ability to grip objects. Difficulty performing daily activities like holding up an object, a cup, opening a jar, or typing
- Rare swelling in the wrist.

CHECKLIST 11.4   SIGNS OF FROZEN SHOULDER OR "ADHESIVE CAPSULITIS"

- Pain in the shoulder at rest or with movement, may worsen over time and may extend to the upper arm.
- Stiffness with increasing limited range of motion due to stiff shoulder joint.
- Increased difficulty with daily activities including brushing hair, washing hair, or reaching up for any objects.
- Limited range of motion and progressive difficulty moving arm and shoulder in certain directions, in front, behind, to the side.
- Pain and discomfort during sleep in any position, including the inability to sleep on the same side as the affected shoulder due to severe pain with pressure.
- Inability to raise both arms symmetrically and straight up.
- For women, inability to zip up the back of dresses or clasp bras.
- Developing numbness, tingling, and/or pain in fingers, hands, or arms.
- Intermittent cyanosis of fingertips, fingers, and hands.
- MRI demonstrating degenerative disks in single or multiple levels, stenosis of cervical foramina, reduced flow of cerebrospinal fluid through foramina.
- Sudden onset severe pain in neck and/or arms.
- Weakness of upper extremity or extremities. Due to a decreased range of motion and decreased use of muscles around the shoulder including the rotator cuff, without surgery or post-surgical decompression, the shoulder joint and muscles become weak.

CHECKLIST 11.5   INTERVENTIONS ONCE NECK/ SHOULDER/ARM PAIN BECOMES FREQUENT OR CHRONIC

- MRI of neck, shoulder, and/or arm, as soon as possible
- Minimize activities that exacerbate pain.
- See an expert orthopedic surgeon with expertise in hand/shoulder. Follow the care plan and recommended exercises. Schedule routine follow-up.

- The orthopedic hand/shoulder specialist can perform in-office injections for carpal tunnel, tennis elbow, frozen shoulder, etc. Not more frequent than at four-month intervals.
- See a neurosurgeon for consultation. Know the extent of your degenerative disc issues and risks.
- Consider cervical epidural corticosteroid injection by an interventional radiologist to reduce swelling/inflammation in the location of the compressed nerves to decrease symptoms and pain. May repeat after the first injection. Ask about side effects.
- Discuss with both your prognosis, indications, risks, rationale, pros, and cons if surgical intervention is recommended.
- Avoid surgery if possible. If recommended, be clear about why and realistic expectations.
- Start physical therapy with excellent PT/DPT, one with experience treating frozen shoulders.
- Lay on the bed with your head supported. Stretch the affected side with arms straight and lift repeatedly over your head and let gravity pull your hand and arm downward. It may hurt. Do this for at least 5 minutes twice a day.

Chapter 12

Delaying Pregnancy, Miscarriage, and Infertility

In May of 2023, I moderated a panel on this rarely discussed topic during the 2023 Annual Meeting of the American Society of Pediatric Otolaryngology. This was the final act and responsibility of my "presidency" for this prestigious national society. I had planned this panel inspired by not only my own traumatic journey but also because of what I learned about the prevalence of these challenges affecting young surgeons in my field. In September 2022, I was a speaker on "Physician Wellbeing" for our American Academy of Otolaryngology Head and Neck Surgery meeting, for the Young Physician Section (YPS) and Section for Residents and Fellows-in-Training (SRF).

Using the audience response system, I asked the hundreds in the audience who had biologically experienced infertility, and 10% responded. The next question I asked was for those who had experienced infertility through their partner or spouses but not themselves biologically, 8% reported they had. So nearly one in five young ENT surgeons had and were dealing with infertility. It's likely the actual numbers are higher as some may not feel comfortable sharing, as this is a highly personal topic, possibly traumatic, and emotionally triggering. When invited to give surgery grand rounds on the topic of physician wellbeing, I always share my infertility struggles to highlight a key topic eroding wellbeing for our trainees and colleagues.

DOI: 10.4324/9781003452478-13   **95**

In Boston, the panel included my dear friends and colleagues; i.e., four female surgeons who practice pediatric otolaryngology. I also had two Ob/GYN physicians and a non-physician fertility counselor who personally endured many miscarriages. One Ob/GYN physician was the Director of Reproductive Endocrinology and Infertility at Brigham and Women's Hospital and Professor of Ob/GYN and Reproductive Biology at Harvard Medical School. He shared his soon-to-be-published research data on trainee attitudes toward fertility and fertility benefits. The other Ob/GYN-turned disability insurance (DI) advisor, shared some insights nearly no medical student or residents and young physicians are aware of: that disability insurance impacts family planning with specific coverage for pregnancy, delivery, infertility, miscarriage, and assisted reproductive technology.

Finally, our non-physician panelist who was a mother, patient, advocate, and author of *The Grace in Grief: Healing and Hope after Miscarriage*[1], spoke about the trauma and healing associated with pregnancy loss. Such devastating loss is rarely discussed nor acknowledged in training environments or professional settings. I moderated with a strong globus sensation while holding back tears, at times unsuccessfully. Our individual and collective grief, suppressed for years related to these challenges, was given the space and overdue compassion in a professional setting where such acknowledgment has not been made.

After our panel, a male pediatric otolaryngologist stepped up to the microphone and thanked us for addressing these topics, he and his wife too, have recently experienced. As I walked out of the ballroom afterward, I was approached by several female otolaryngologists. Most were tearful and grateful and shared how validating our stories were. They too experience the unspoken pain, shame, and trauma of infertility, miscarriage, and delaying pregnancy. I received texts of similar messages from other colleagues, several are highly visible in our subspecialty but also suffered privately and have carried their pain despite professional success. This is a subject that must be addressed for otolaryngology at large as we emphasize the need to achieve gender, racial, and ethnic equity for our workforce. So many female surgeons have grieved in silence for decades, but we can create positive change to support current female, and male, otolaryngology residents, fellows, and any faculty who have or are struggling regardless of programs, geography, and subspecialties.

Rangel et al. reported in 2021 a staggering 42% out of 692 female surgeons surveyed had experienced pregnancy loss, over twice the rate for the general population.[2] Compared to male surgeons, female surgeons have fewer children (1.8 vs 2.3), are more likely to delay having children due to training (65% vs 32%) and are more likely to use ART to achieve pregnancy (24.9% vs 17.1%). Compared to the non-surgeon partners of their colleagues, female surgeons are more likely to experience major pregnancy complications (48.3% vs 27.2%), experience musculoskeletal disorders (36.9% vs 18.4%, addressed by one of our keynote speakers Dr. Geeta Lal and our panel on surgical ergonomics). Female surgeons are more likely to undergo non-elective C-section (25.5% vs 15.3%) and experience post-partum depression (11.1% vs 5.7%).

Another study by *Champaloux et al.* from 2022, "Otolaryngology residents' experience of pregnancy and return to work: A multisite qualitative study", reported 37.5% of female otolaryngologists who experienced miscarriages or complications during their pregnancy in residency.[3] The semi-structured confidential interviews and thematic analysis of transcripts shared the theme of leadership bias against pregnancy for female otolaryngology residents, and some factors which contribute to unhealthy postpartum period include smaller programs, lengthy cases, disruption in breast milk pumping, lack of child-bearing role models, and lack of stay-at-home partners or family support. Those who had such support were able to return to work earlier.

In this anonymous survey of trainees to assess fertility knowledge and the impact of employer coverage for fertility services, my expert panelist shared updated definitions. Recurrent pregnancy loss is defined by two or more miscarriages. Infertility is defined as not conceiving after 12 months of unprotected intercourse in women less than age 35, or six months in women aged 35 and older. Currently, only 18 states have infertility insurance mandates but not all cover IVF.

Our Ob/GYN insurance advisor shared with the audience the following:

- Higher socioeconomic status is associated with greater use of fertility treatments.
- Every woman should get a DI policy in place before trying for her first pregnancy.
- If spontaneous abortion occurs within 12 months of applying, this results in the exclusion of coverage.
- If infertility is listed on the records, this too results in the exclusion of coverage.
- The abnormal outcome of pregnancy results in the exclusion of coverage.
- When asked if one has used artificial reproductive technology in the past or currently, even if one pays out of pocket, this must be disclosed honestly and will likely result in exclusion of coverage.

Having a DI policy in place is crucial, as that impacts protection for all surgeons and physicians who suffer injury due to surgical ergonomics, but also potential coverage for infertility and miscarriages. Given that research shows female surgeons are at higher risk for Work Related Musculoskeletal Disorders/injury, infertility, miscarriage, complications associated with birth, and postpartum depression, my hope is for all readers of this article to support trainees and young faculty so that they will secure DI policy as soon as possible.

Here is my story. I didn't get married until six months after completing a two-year fellowship in pediatric otolaryngology, right before my 33rd birthday. As I am almost five years older than my husband, I knew I was ready to start a family and have a child pretty much as soon as we were married, but we shared a different sense of urgency. I was grateful to have found a spouse and partner, a chance to be married, and begin my "real job" as an attending. Buying our first house together (my first) and finally living the generic "dream" by all trainees, did not include any warnings that I would endure primary infertility and later secondary infertility, after a miracle pregnancy.

My husband rarely reminds me of my unfair tactic of playing the "dead mother card" as he describes it. I do recall the day when I absolutely wanted to change his mind, and stop waiting to try and have a child, despite having been married a little over a year. I told him that had my mother, who died of breast cancer when I was nine and a half, known she would be forced to leave me, she would have tried to have me earlier in her life so that she could spend more time with me. Yes, that was warped, but I wanted a baby. My husband also lost his mother during freshman year in college, as a drunk driver took her life. He gave in.

Claire was my miracle pregnancy. After a year of being told first to simply wait, then months of Clomid, daily temperature checks, excruciatingly painful hysterosalpingogram, husband's sperm analysis, intrauterine inseminations, acupuncture for pregnancy, a fertility diet, time, and expense led only to labs indicating I had low "ovarian reserve". Why didn't anyone tell me that? They didn't teach us that in medical school. How does one preserve their ovarian reserve? If I had known I would have done whatever it took to maintain and protect my "reserve".

The consultations, appointments, and procedures are a blur amidst realities of busy clinical, OR schedules, teaching, research, and other professional activities "achieve". Eventually, my parents found a rare fertility-specific, Buddhist Goddess of Compassion or "Guan-Yin" after an exhaustive search in Chinatown stores in Los Angeles. They brought her to us in Kansas City. She holds an infant, much like statues of the Virgin Mary holding baby Jesus. I found out I was pregnant a few weeks later. This actual Guan-Yin statue and those like it, have helped several colleagues, my cousins, and other women who endure infertility struggles.

We tried to have more children but were never successful. By the time Claire was two, I had undergone consultations with "top" fertility experts in Kansas City, told my only choice was to use an egg donor but there were only seven in the Kansas City area. We were uncomfortable with the chance our child may grow up meeting half-siblings in that city or area. We found one willing to support my desire to try IVF. I will never forget carrying many syringes as I traveled to present at an ASPO meeting. I am so fearful of needles, yet endured the scheduled self-injections and would have endured far more to achieve another pregnancy. I rushed home on a Sunday after the COSM meeting, excited and naïve as Monday was egg retrieval and then we would finally have that second baby I wanted so desperately. During the egg harvest procedure, the ultrasound technician was quiet and appeared to be confused. When I finally asked what was wrong, she said "I can't find your right ovary". How does one lose an ovary? IVF was not possible as not a single egg was found for retrieval from the lonely left ovary.

For a couple of years after, while building busy clinical practices, building my academic resume, service to hospitals and societies, teaching, and conducting clinical trials, we spent more time considering using egg donors and/or surrogates. I even completed papers for adoption couple right before completing my Triological Thesis. Eventually being consumed by work and career, amidst a high degree of burnout, but with great joy from our Claire, I stopped feeling the pain.

My colleagues and I shared our stories that day and now in a journal article, in hopes of increasing collective awareness, creating permission to address shame, pain, and suffering for our colleagues, but most importantly inspiring actions across otolaryngology training programs to support and help trainees and younger faculty.[4] To achieve physician wellbeing and healing, we must acknowledge our trauma and suffering from infertility and miscarriage. Delaying pregnancy during training or at any time should be a well-informed choice with DI policy in place, not a decision made out of fear of the stigma and bias against pregnancy in female physicians. Women physicians, trainees, and medical students deserve to be celebrated and empowered to celebrate themselves and support one another when they achieve pregnancy and create new lives.

CHECKLIST 12.1   KNOW YOU ARE NOT ALONE

- Between 15% and 20% of clinically recognized pregnancies end in miscarriage (pregnancy loss earlier than 20 weeks of gestation). This is even higher for female physicians and especially surgeons. Advancing maternal age is one of several factors.
- There remains much misconception about the prevalence and causes of miscarriage.
- Keeping the miscarriage a secret does not help with the processing of grief and/or healing.
- Take time off if you suffered a miscarriage, an event which impacts women physically, emotionally, mentally, and even spiritually beyond

the religious sense. Loss and grief are real, and require no explanation to others, nor justification. Make time and space for mourning, processing, and healing. Take short-term disability (up to six weeks).

- Talk to a counselor, set up multiple sessions, and as many as needed.
- Take time to ensure your own health is optimal as several medical conditions can increase the risk of miscarriage such as uncontrolled diabetes, thyroid disease, and any uterine or cervical problems.
- If it's not your first miscarriage, seek out a reproductive endocrinology expert and someone familiar with reproductive immunology.
- If you have experienced pregnancy loss, read *The Grace in Grief* by Laura Fletcher.

CHECKLIST 12.2   WHAT YOU MAY NOT KNOW

- Get disability insurance as early as possible, in medical school, residency, or by fellowship training. The goal is to have it in place BEFORE any attempt to get pregnant.
- Find out if your state is one that mandates insurance coverage for reproductive health and fertility treatments.
- For female physicians and especially surgeons aged 30 or higher, or anytime you are ready to start a family, don't let your Ob/GYN or anyone tell you to just "wait". Ovarian reserve continues to decrease over time and is negatively influenced by stress, lifestyle, and other factors.
- If you are a trainee, you may already experience bias when announcing your pregnancy, or be afraid to become pregnant due to your program and leadership bias. Speak to someone at your institution, any women physician leaders outside your training program, or to a physician leader at your institution's ACGME office, Associate Dean for Graduate Medical Education (GME), etc.
- Speak collectively within your residency training program so that all female residents can share openly and support one another regarding your individual plans and concerns. Once you can share and support one another, also involve male co-residents as some will likely have spouses/partners that have children and thus have shared concerns about having children during training.

- For trainees, identify and engage at least one or more highly supportive faculty especially a female faculty, then as a group, you will have a stronger voice to ensure department-wide policies and culture that support instead of penalizing trainless who want to start a family during residency or fellowship.
- Plan and take parental leave as needed, or any type of leave as needed, to care for family members/loved ones, dealing with PTSD/mental health issues, own medical health issues, etc. Contact your GME office and institutional HR department to understand the leave policy and how to activate leave.
- For trainees, a recently published study in ophthalmology highlighted no difference between the performance metrics of those who took parental leave vs those who didn't.[5] You should not assume if you take leave you will have to delay residency graduation. Speak to your Program Director (PD) and chair to discuss the best options.
- As of November 2022, the AMA House of Delegates consensus recommendation is for programs to provide up to 12 weeks of paid leave in a 12-month period for attendings and trainees as needed (AMA).[6]

Chapter 13

How to "Off-Ramp", "On-Ramp", or Exit Your Clinical Career – Safely

I was recently honored as an invited speaker for an endowed lectureship, speaking of a course on "Work-Life Integration, Physician Wellbeing and Safety". What a gift to be a part of an academic otolaryngology department for their annual meeting as well as their residency graduation celebrating the young men and women who have completed surgical training. As always, when I share about my own PTSD like trauma from a career in surgery, describing the circumstance and experience always triggers visceral emotions and tears. Authenticity is experienced by others anytime we speak our truths and share vulnerabilities.

At the end of the presentation, I was sincerely moved by the standing ovation from the audience of my otolaryngology peers. A surgeon in the audience asked me for my recommendations and thoughts on what physicians and surgeons should do in preparation for retirement. His question was prefaced with a profound anecdote: an anesthesia colleague who had an impactful career, had retired, but within two years committed suicide. The basis for his question is related to just how strong our identity is to our career and profession, and that when we stop doing what we have done for decades, losing sense of purpose for life can be a risk for any physician.

Before I gave my answer, I asked the audience to raise their hands if they had personally known a physician who had committed suicide. Near a dozen hands went up. In every one of my presentations, I highlight the continued epidemic of

DOI: 10.4324/9781003452478-14

over 400 physician suicides per year, with surgeons and anesthesiologists as the top two specialties at risk.

I am unaware of any standardized curriculum or professional guidance physicians are ever given, by their employer, medical staff office, professional societies, or other forums that support physicians as they reach or near retirement age. How can physicians "off-ramp" safely? What actions should they take in planning their future when the time comes as planned or prematurely for them to decrease or stop practicing clinical medicine?

When searching the definition of "off-ramp", one finds that it is defined as a ramp or exit by which one leaves a limited-access highway. Another definition includes a short road that is used to gradually slow down after leaving a highway. In business, the terms "off-ramps" and "on-ramps" refer to when individuals leave or enter the workforce, respectively. As I searched articles on this topic, it was quickly apparent to me that two separate topics need to be explored. One is that specific to women, while the broader focus is one for all physicians.

Harvard Business Review published in 2005, *Off-Ramps and On-Ramps: Keeping Talented Women On the Road to Success*, highlighting the "opt-out" revolution observed as many highly qualified women were dropping out of mainstream careers, ranging from 57% women graduates from the class of 1981 at Stanford, to 38% women graduates from three graduating classes at Harvard Business School ending up in full-time careers[1]. During the past two decades, I have witnessed and participated in intentional efforts to increase diversity based on gender, race, and ethnicity. Additionally, the need to address pay equity, and professional and career development for women has been published and noted across surgical subspecialties given that female surgeons have historically been underrepresented for a variety of reasons. This chapter highlights the same issues exacerbated by the pandemic, women opting out due to demands of caring for children, elderly parents, other family members, personal health issues, none of which has anything to do with women's desire to pursue and realize their career potential despite similar investment of time, cost, and energy in their education and training.

What was eye-opening was reading the contrasting top five reasons men and women leave the "fast lane" according to survey results conducted by the Center for Work-Life Policy in 2001.[1] Twenty-five years ago, 40% of highly qualified women with spouses felt their husbands create more work around the house than they perform! Yet for highly qualified women who were off-ramped, 93% intended and wanted to return to their careers – the key reason being financial as women want their own independent source of income as well as cited household or partner's income being insufficient for family needs. Of course, many return to work seeking enjoyment and satisfaction from their careers as well as having a strong desire to contribute to their communities and society at large.

I emphasize the moral injustice facing many female physicians today, as they are not given permission nor support, to temporarily "off-ramp" due to demands they alone must meet that are not of their own choosing. In the business of healthcare, I have heard too many times and witnessed the absolute ignorance of those who influence physician realities to uphold "gender blindness" and dismiss conversations or any possibilities for highly committed and talented female physicians to take time off, work less than full-time, have every aspect of their contributions "count" as work instead of only clinical work and "RVUs" being acknowledged as "real work", and all other financially driven parameters that define their careers and work.

The expectation has always been that unless it's maternity leave, female physicians should never take leave or work less than full time and if they do, they will be penalized in both compensation, and stigma, and denied any leadership and career advancement opportunities. In the current healthcare culture, it appears for many female physicians, maternity leave is the only acceptable nuisance for employers as there is a great impact on the bottom line.

Perhaps if more mid- and senior male physicians started taking leaves of absence, not related to terminal illness or diagnoses, or debilitating injuries, and not just the young physicians today who embrace paternity leave, I believe we can jumpstart a cultural *SHIFT* and achieve greater career longevity as alluded to in earlier chapter. Another risk rarely discussed of relevance for physicians who are more senior, likely near 60 or older, is the risk of implicit age discrimination based on the higher salaries older physicians enjoy. They may be the ones forced to resign, asked to retire early, or facing a reduction in force. Any physician may be forced to resign due to politically motivated, or other reasons independent of clinical competence and patient-related matters. Such circumstances are not only emotionally devastating but have a direct impact on not only the physician but all their dependents and family if they don't already have clear financial plans and actions taken to protect against loss of income and employment. The greatest risk for anyone to stop working before age 65 is the loss of health insurance coverage before qualifying for Medicare.

I have created checklists below for what female physicians should consider when they choose or feel forced to work part-time for their own benefit or that of others. Just as importantly, checklists are needed to help every physician consider, ahead of nearing retirement age, how to transition away from clinical care so that they can finally enjoy time experiencing many aspects of themselves without feeling "lost" or losing a sense of purpose for living.

Each physician will have a different roadmap, but all deserve to get off the "highway" of their careers where there seems to no longer be speed limits, greater risk for accidents and injury, lack of rest stops and service stations, and even when wheels come off one is expected to maintain same speed without a destination in sight. But first, physicians must learn how to see themselves as holistic human beings, and recognize that by deferring to make and choose time and energy to invest in hobbies, relationships with loved ones and friends, engagement in activities aligned with their core values outside of medicine and surgery, and equally important learn how to sit still or simply "be" without being "productive", taking any "exit" will feel uncomfortable and even distressing, if they haven't charted out their own map of the adventures that awaits them which hopefully are taken before losing physical health and cognitive capacity.

CHECKLIST 13.1   FIRST, GET TO KNOW YOU SO YOU CAN LIVE YOUR BEST LIFE OUTSIDE AND AFTER CLINICAL PRACTICE

- If I asked your spouse or partners, and it was up to them, how much more time each day, and what activities would he/she/they wish they could enjoy with you, for their "perfect day?"
- If I asked your children, and it was up to them, how much more time, how frequent, and what activities would they wish you were available for, for them and their children (your grandchildren) if they have any?
- When you fantasize about a single day without work, what would you declare you would want? Sleep in? Get up early? Read the newspaper? Nap? Walk? Read more?
- What are your current hobbies? Favorite activities? Include all, physical exercise, and any activity that involves you NOT being a physician.
- Are you currently spending as much time as you'd like on your favorite hobbies?
- In your ideal or "perfect" day, how frequently and how much time would you spend on each of your favorite hobbies or activities?
- Write out your "perfect" day from the time you wake up until you go to sleep – if NOT at work or practicing clinical medicine. Create several versions as you wish, with various activities you choose, and include who you would spend time with for any activities.
- Do you believe you are currently at your best health? If not, what are your current health challenges? What have you done to improve your health? What have you been told by physicians or others as critical changes to improve your health?

- If you are not healthy, why have you NOT made the critical changes you know and your physicians have told you will result in the greatest improvements in your health?
- If you are not healthy, write out how the lack of physical health will impact your life once you transition out of full-time or part-time clinical practice.
- Have you met with your financial advisor recently to specifically focus on reviewing your current financial portfolio, assets, and debts, and confirmed when you can retire based on what you and your partner/spouse (if any) hope as the lifestyle you want after you stop working?
- What would you worry about the most if you walked away from clinical practice today? Are the concerns specific to you, your family members, colleagues, and patients, who and how?
- Have you discussed your concerns with anyone else? Are your concerns valid or perceptions based on assumptions?
- Which relationships and interactions do you enjoy the most outside of work? Individuals or groups. Do you feel you have invested enough time and energy into these relationships?
- Who are the people in your lives that you would like to see more and spend more time with? Outside of work settings.
- What hobbies or activities have you neglected, given up, regret not doing more of, or have never tried, since entering medical school and working as a physician?
- What topics do you find yourself wanting to read more about?
- What community or volunteer services and activities have you participated in recently or ever? How did you feel when you were participating in such services and activities?
- Are there any groups of people who are non-physicians, that you enjoy interacting with? Have you missed out on recurrent gatherings or activities by such groups due to being a physician and working?
- Where have you traveled? How many countries, continents, and places with a language you don't speak?
- What epic trip would you like to experience if you have money, time, and even company to go with? Safari? Rain forest? Scuba diving? Remote island? Antarctica? Food-focused travel in Italy, Spain, France, or any European country? Dream golf course to play?

- What is your favorite sports team? Which sport, which team? Where are they? Have you ever been to an event/game of that team?
- Who is your favorite band? What is your favorite type of music? Opera? Plays? Broadway? Musicals? Comedian?
- What festivals have you heard about anywhere in the US and internationally that you have thought about, or are interested in experiencing? Food, music, any theme-related, cultural, or religious festivals?
- Have you traveled more, or less, than you had envisioned for your life? With your partner/spouse?
- Do you have a bucket list of activities and/or travel? When was the last time you reviewed or updated it?
- What do you need to know or plan, in order to start planning travel or whatever it was to start tackling your "bucket" list of wishes? Who are the people that show up on your bucket list?
- Have you discussed with HR, your employer, and your immediate supervisor, your timing for reduced clinical work or retirement?
- Do you know exactly what benefits you will have at and after your retirement or reduced clinical practice? Health insurance, pension, cashing out PTO, even severance in case you get laid off.
- What do you like to read? Books? News? Magazines? Fiction? Non-fiction?
- Have you and your spouse/partner ever talked about what single or few activities you would want to try or learn, and do together, if you could?
- If you struggle with having few answers to each of the above, try spending some time searching on the internet, YouTube, and check out videos, images, and websites of these topics and start to think about what you would enjoy, as well as that of your partner or spouse.

CHECKLIST 13.2   CONSIDERATIONS FOR TEMPORARY "TIME OUT" OR "OFF-RAMP"

- Why do you want or need time off? Who is it for?
- What are the exact challenges for your current life demands that working full time with your current schedule is unsustainable or undesirable for you? No need to justify, just list.

- What would your daily and weekly schedule look like to accommodate your life demands which require a reduction in hours worked in your current situation?
- Does each day have to look the same? Write out every day of the week, clinic, OR, admin, research, whatever days, wherever you are (main hospital or satellite clinic, or home clinic base), so you know exactly what that schedule is to be your near-perfect schedule.
- Be clear and do not over-exaggerate time needed nor underestimate time needed away from work.
- Are such demands requiring you to reduce clinical work temporarily or semi-permanently? For how long?
- What resources and alternatives are necessary in order for you to offload, if you wanted to, such demands so that you could work 1.0 FTE (full time equivalent) or full time if you wanted to?
- Have you discussed and explored such alternatives and resources with your spouse, partner, family members, financial advisors, friends, or whomever is necessary in your life to support such demands?
- What is the financial impact to you and your family, if you take a leave or "time out"?
- How long can you afford to reduce your hours or take time off? What is the impact on your budget and monthly expenses or savings? What would you have to give up due to a decrease in salary?
- Other than salary, what else will you have to "give up" or "sacrifice", or even possibly be "penalized" should you stop working full time or ask for a temporarily reduction in clinical efforts and work schedule?
- Who do you know and trust, with experience, that you can share your current dilemma and challenges with, and review your "fantasy" schedule with, as well as impact, and give you sound advice or suggestions that you may not have thought of?
- Do you know your "boss" and employer/organization well enough, and their HR policy, to know if they will support your ask? Or do you already know you have to be prepared to fight and be denied?
- What is the likelihood that any leadership role(s) or titles will be taken from you, if you take temporarily time out or reduce clinical effort? Are you willing to still make that decision knowing this possibility?

- Write out a clear document, outline reasons WHY you need this "break", and WHY your boss/employer should support you. Provide the most realistic and reasonable offers you can make in exchange, whether it be longevity in service once you return to work, commitment to staying and not considering change in employment, any activities you are able to do if given more flexibility, to contribute to the needs of your group, division, department, or asks from your employer that your "fantasy" schedule allows without compromising your priorities.
- Make an appointment with your supervisor or whomever you need to make this request in person. Practice this conversation many times before the meeting.
- Review your employer's HR policy related to leave, and state and federal laws that may be applicable before your meeting.
- Be prepared to hear "no", regardless of reason, and be very prepared NOT to acquiesce and accept "NO".
- Prepare to ask repeatedly WHY NOT if you are denied and how you would end that conversation and exit the room.
- Be clear that you are there to discuss the best options that support your needs as well as the employer and group's needs, with minimal and reasonable/unavoidable impact on patients and practice.
- Do you know the impact on your pay and benefits? Are there options for you to have your leave covered by full or partial salary?
- What is your BATNA? Best alternative to a negotiated agreement? Is the circumstance bad enough that if you simply hear "NO" without any flexibility or option, are you prepared to leave? Have you looked at other options for employment? Have you interviewed elsewhere for other job opportunities? Have you discussed with your spouse/partner, counselor, anyone, and most of all yourself, if you are at the right job with the right people, the right culture, the right environment, at this time?
- Be prepared to offer plan B if plan A is absolutely not acceptable for your employer. You don't need to offer plan B during the same meeting. Instead, end the meeting by requesting the person to consider your needs and schedule a follow-up meeting.

CHECKLIST 13.3   CONSIDERATIONS FOR RETURNING TO WORK OR "ON-RAMP"

- Anxiety is normal so expect it, acknowledge it but don't let it be a squatter.
- Feeling like "what if" I can't, I don't like it, it will be difficult, or I will be uncomfortable, or whatever your inner voice is, hear it once, and tell it to shut up if it's not constructive.
- What would be best for you? Slow return or return immediately to full schedule?
- What, if any, special accommodations do you need in order to return to work successfully and safely? Any temporary or permanent accommodations for your work duties?
- If you need special accommodations, does your employer, team, and supervisor know what they are and have they agreed to them?
- Have your job demands or work environments and resources to do your work changed while you were gone? Without your awareness or discussion? If so what are they? Who would you ask to find out?
- How long will you need accommodations in the schedule or whatever else, until you can return to work without any special accommodations in time, schedule, resources?
- It's okay for things not to go smoothly for the first day, week, or month.
- Allow frustrations but examine them, what are they based on?
- Ask your supervisor and teammates what you missed while out on leave or on break.
- Ask others what they would like you to consider on your return, that is related to their greatest concern or wishes to help their current work demands.
- Who are in your life outside of work that you have asked and prepared to help you return to work so that you can focus on work?
- What are your backup mechanisms in case of family crises? i.e., neighbor, friend, carpool, extended family members, hired help who can provide child or elder parent care, pet care.

Chapter 14

What Hospitals, Health Systems, Academic Institutions Can and Should Do to Ensure Healthy Physician Workforce

---

The cost of physician turnover is as much as 4.6 billion a year according to a recent study.[1] *Harvard Business Review* has been often cited in healthcare as a highly respected source covering topics in management, operations, leadership, negotiations, strategy, marketing, finance, and other relevant issues across industries. Yet when HBR states what other industries should learn about preventing burnout from healthcare, that's not the flattery those in healthcare seek or enjoy.[2]

Despite physician salaries and physicians being perceived as the highest line of "expense" in any hospital or health system financial ledger, and even with the promise of a changed future by using ChatGPT, physicians are needed and not easily replaceable for their unique expertise and immeasurable value from years of experience especially needed to treat the more complicate and even life-threatening conditions. As much as employers can balance their budgets easily by using lower-salaried alternate "providers" such as physician assistants, nurse practitioners, and nurse anesthetists, those valued roles and their contributions are complementary, augment, and critical to increasing patient access but simply do not replace physicians with their years of training and knowledge required for board certification.

What the public nor employers seem to realize is that while an employer can always post a vacant position, advertise to recruit, and then spend months to years recruiting, every disruption or physician leaving his/her/their clinic, hospital, system, or place of "business" impact thousands of patients by decreasing patient access, increasing wait time to appointments, not to mention loss of the relationship built on trust over time and several visits as well as the intangibles that still matter to BOTH the patients and the physicians. For the emphasis placed on "productivity" by healthcare employers and systems, it seems intuitive and logical that healthy physicians and those who feel appreciated, respected, and cared for will also be the ones to achieve high productivity as a secondary focus as they provide high-quality and safe care.

Of course, this appears logical from a physician's perspective, but perhaps from a non-physician business perspective, such a notion is deemed not possible or there exists a narrative that to make physicians "happy" is not affordable, not worth the return on investment, or not possible. The physician workforce should be treated as the marital partner of any employer in healthcare, instead of the "help". While physicians are entitled and some will choose to move and leave the employer for family and personal reasons, far more have left for poor value alignment, or reaching a point of believing that their departure is the ultimate self-preserving action against either a toxic environment, or one with unsustainable stress without support, or one where change for a more positive culture is not possible.

Finally, the physician workforce, individually and collectively, should never be underestimated in their abilities and interest to contribute to the change instead of "waiting" for it to make things better for themselves, the patients, and the public at large. Negative bias against physicians as potential outstanding leaders in healthcare, narratives that they should "stick" to their "doctor" duties and leave the business to non-physician executives, is frankly an attitude that will unlikely accelerate any hospital or system toward success across strategic goals and metrics. Frankly, a dissatisfied and/or unfulfilled physician can become a source of energy drain and even disruptive, which can have a significant negative impact on the "troubled" physician, team members, staff, and patients.

CHECKLIST 14.1 EMPLOYER RESPONSIBILITIES AND OPPORTUNITIES TO RECRUIT AND RETAIN TALENT, MINIMIZE PATIENT SAFETY RISKS, AND MAXIMIZE PHYSICIAN ENGAGEMENT

- Embed psychologists into medical staff, hospitals, and health systems.
- Create an immediate access line and focus on a culture that encourages medical staff, trainees, and faculty to use the line as often as needed. The single phone number should be answered by psychologists 24/7/365, without completing the intake process, and paperwork, or waiting for a call back the next day or whenever. Such a line is intended to support immediate needs during traumatic events at work, failed resuscitations, triggering events, emotional distress, experiencing sentinel events, and/or personal life challenges of any kind.
- Clear access to counseling for all medical staff who activate or use the immediate access line.
- Options for physicians, especially women, to choose part-time work without penalty, and willingness to compromise and engage in conversations about what's possible, the duration of such arrangements, and criteria and metrics required for supporting such arrangements including commitment to stay longer term with the employer in exchange of flexibility for the desired period.
- Supportive conditions to allow physicians to return to work after FMLA or any leave of absence, easily and without experiencing implicit or explicit bias.
- Leaders should send the message loud and clear, from the top or C-suite, to all administrators and managers (especially non-physicians), that the human needs of physicians matter. Leaders should refrain from a negative narrative when physicians should and must spend time away from work for appropriate reasons, without the stigma of punitive actions for negative impact on RVUs.
- Normalize counseling by having executive leaders in healthcare participate or model the use of counseling themselves or specific support above and beyond EAP.
- Overhaul simplistic measure of physician productivity and narrated "value" to an employer using Relative Value Units (RVUs). Collaborate with physician leaders on understanding how to value physicians holistically. RVUs and other metrics including financial,

are simply one of many aspects of their contribution to the operational impact on any hospital and system.

■ Adopting Schwartz Rounds for compassionate healthcare with a focus on supporting frontline workers including doctors and nurses.[3]

■ Stop the annual engagement surveys unless hospital executive leaders have the means and intention to address the issues. Physicians and other employees really resent spending time completing surveys, including lengthy free texts to articulate their concerns and dissatisfaction, trying not to have their hopes up that concerns will be addressed, just to have their fear proven by silence and lack of any communication or action-based plans by the leadership after any survey has been completed.

■ Share transparently with the entire physician workforce, turnover rates, and costs over the years in your system.

■ Change physician compensation and bonus structure to incentivize quality and education, the key areas that a system has declared publicly they prioritize OVER productivity metrics. For example, do not tell physicians that research, external funding, academic ranking, and national reputation matter, when a bonus achievable beyond the RVU threshold is unlimited while other activities may or may not result in any incentive pay. Not to mention, if there are no protected time, funds, or mentorship and other resources to devote to such said activities. Magic simply does not occur where expectations keep rising without the necessary time and resources.

■ Incentives should be structured relative to the reality of the patient population served. For example, if physicians and the workforce rely on discretionary effort for disproportionately high patient populations with language barriers, social determinants of health challenges, poverty, medical complexity, government insurance, and complex comorbidities requiring greater care plan and communication, then this must be accounted for instead of expect "productivity" and financial performance as if the majority of patients are insured by commercial payors, healthy, routine, and without real-life challenges that impact health.

■ Using metrics that aren't achievable given your hospital and system's reality, i.e., lack of resources, staffing, physical space for office exam rooms or operating rooms, not having access to a surgery center, lacking efficiency or workflow infrastructure, technology, IT support and platforms, lack of investment in technology, yet still expecting high throughput.

- Hold administrators to high levels of accountability and subject them to metrics around physician satisfaction and turnover.
- Do not lie to a physician. Do not mislead, misinform, or withhold information, key data, and/or any other relevant information they deserve and want to know, when making critical decisions about clinical services they are expected to provide and depth of coverage.
- Physicians react negatively to services they have been promised to deliver, by administration and others, without being informed first nor having a chance to discuss how realistic, how soon, how well, and if they can do so without compromising the quality of care and how they want to deliver that care. A parallel would be promising your daughter to a family she will marry that she has never met, and that she will do all the housework, cook, clean, and change her profession and job based on whatever her husband wants regardless of what she wants. Another parallel is perhaps you promising to fix your friend's car by tomorrow night, but you have no mechanical training and you have no time until next week or month to even go visit your friend.
- Avoid laying off physicians while sending out emails congratulating multiple non-physicians on their promotion to titles including "vice president", "senior vice president", or whatever promotion without any context nor transparency on the impact on system expenses for salary adjustments.
- Provide easy access to coffee, tea, fresh fruit, and snacks and make them accessible. Such will improve mood and productivity. A "hangry" physician and surgeon are not good for anyone. Even if they brought their own lunch or snacks, often they never had time to consume them.
- Consistently and transparently share annual turnover data, exit interview findings, reasons for departure, as well as summary and data from surveys for those who choose to stay. Both will help physicians understand instead of making up their own narratives, even if true. If you aren't willing, ready, or able to do this, ask WHY.
- If your organization's physician turnover rate is higher than the national average, executive leaders should have a clear understanding of key factors and reasons as well as action plans to address and reverse the trend. Leaving this as simply an HR function, or ignoring it, has far broader consequences. Physicians talk to one another, across hospitals and institutions, stateliness, and as neighbors and moms whose children go to the same schools or activities. A negative reputation will not help recruitment efforts or costs.

- When mistakes are made in strategy, implementation, or poor communication, apologize to physicians. Acknowledge issues and mistakes, and demonstrate you care about the impact on physicians.
- Beware of public or private comments made by executive leaders (especially non-physicians) that are negatively biased, condescending, unprofessional, and reflect a total lack of respect toward physicians. Many in your own institutions hear such remarks, and you would be surprised how many know and the culture it reflects. Not helpful for recruiting top talents for your organization's key physician leadership roles.
- Whatever the financial challenges and issues are, do not assume physicians don't care, don't understand, nor are willing to help address them with administrators and financial officers.
- Avoid telling physicians they had input or that they were involved in a decision, when in fact they were informed after the decision was made. They know the difference.
- Try and understand, and more importantly, appreciate the clinical programs your physicians and teams have built and how they impact your patients, communities served, and hospital and organizational standing. Even if the leaders are not clinical, they can ask others in similar roles at other institutions to have deeper appreciation and respect for their own talented workforce.
- Be realistic and understand when physicians express concern over coverage. Patient safety will be at risk when high-risk areas including OR, anesthesia, any intensive care units, or any services are inadequately staffed against patient volume already served, transfers, expansive regional coverage, and contracted services offered by the hospital.
- Hiring advanced practice providers, anesthesia associates, and CRNAs (Certified Registered Nurse Anesthetist) can absolutely augment your total workforce. But they require training and great leadership to work seamlessly in a single team culture. They are NOT solutions to replacing physicians in budgeting exercises.
- Quality in your hires does matter. Having a terrible hire, even as a locum, will have negative consequences for the team and quality of care, and a negative impact on the reputation in the community. Bad care travels faster on mommy Facebook page and support groups. Patients have choices and you already know the competition in your markets.

- Do not enable, deny, or excuse unprofessional and unacceptable behavior by any physician or anyone, including and especially surgeons, regardless of how much revenue they bring to the hospital and how much their program accounts for hospital income. The negative impacts on the lives, not just on patients but on those in your hospital, doctors, nurses, or any team members they hurt, insult, or abuse, or those that threaten the psychological safety of others, are immeasurable. If you are covering up patient safety issues to protect the revenue stream, it will be a matter of time before issues will come to light.

- Demonstrate that executive leadership does not tolerate implicit or explicit bias in its management, nonphysician, and administrative workforce. Anyone who makes comments that are unprofessional and reflect bias against gender, race, ethnicity, and/or all other biases should be addressed with performance management plans. Bullying or targeting of specific physicians or groups, including misogynistic attitudes, should not be tolerated in healthcare administration.

- Consider a physician's need and impact on patients when creating and enforcing restrictive covenants to his/her/their practice. For many, physicians rely on the ability to practice to financially support their own families, pay back educational loans, ensure access to health insurance, and may support elderly parents who were moved to your city so that the physician can work for you in the first place. The enforcing of restrictive covenant simply to protect "market" share is outrageous. Patients don't care about "market share", they care about ability to continue seeing the physicians they trust and receive great care from.

- Achieving short-term financial goals and budgets at the expense of current and long-term viability and financial success of your hospital, health system, and most of all your workforce, will unlikely lead to a strong future. Consequences and struggles in workforce turnover, unnecessary financial losses due to turnover, paying extra for labor for travelers and/or locums, new hires, onboarding, continued decreased workforce engagement, and organizational reputation, safety issues, are avoidable. The strongest of systems are likely led by those who can think differently, stop using same decades old tactics and strategies, or same strategies a consulting firm has offered to dozens of hospitals as their clients.

- Consider creating physician roles across various areas of your hospital and system operations, IT, Finance, Billing/Coding/revenue cycle, centralized scheduling, EPIC/EHR, marketing and communications, HR, employee health, and countless other areas that traditionally do not have physician voices and input. This is in addition to traditional medical staff committees and functionality.
- Consider having C-suite executives each with open "office hours" for physicians to walk in without appointment, 10–15 minutes, to share greatest concerns or feedback for C-suite leaders.
- Thank physicians in ways they can experience and want. Most physicians are busy in clinical care so doctor's day luncheon or activities aren't widely enjoyed by most. Those in OR, satellite clinics, primary care offices, they miss the "celebratory" activities at the hospital. Always feels like salt has been poured into a gaping wound to see social media posts of hospital events celebrating physicians when majority were unable to participate.
- Allow PTO to roll over, bring in massage therapists to OR lounge and breakrooms in intensive care units, give extra hours of PTO or discretionary mental health day, car washing, meal delivery, flexibility for those with childcare needs, some other form of gifts that they need and benefit from to achieve work–life integration and better wellbeing.
- Surprise them. Just as many spouses and partners enjoy a well-planned surprise, an act that demonstrates thought and effort were given to make one feel special, this can be done for physicians.
- Ask and never assume what a physician is thinking or feeling. Worse, never assume physicians don't know, don't care, don't understand.

Chapter 15

Checklist for Optimal Future of US Healthcare

CHECKLIST 15.1   POSSIBLE ACTIONS TO IMPROVE US
HEALTHCARE DELIVERY AND SYSTEMS AS EXPERIENCED
BY PHYSICIANS AND PATIENTS

- Acknowledge the reality and negative impacts and unintended consequences of widespread mandatory adoption and use of electronic
  medical records.
- Ensure organizations and employers have a robust number of electronic medical record analysts and infrastructure to create tools and
  workflow that optimize physician workflow efficiency, streamlined
  workflow, and reduce redundant or non-value-added work and simply,
  the number of keyboard "clicks" needed for every patient encounter.
- Leverage technology and expertise, including the use of appropriate
  and reliable healthcare related artificial intelligence (AI), with physician input, to simplify documentation without sacrificing critical
  patient information for acute and future care.
- Leverage AI to reduce work that does not require human intelligence,
  experience, and expertise, and AI to enhance predictive analytics that

reduce stress while enhancing physician productivity and ability to practice to scope.

■ Increase efficiency of as many aspects and components of patient interface with healthcare regardless of setting, acuity, and with their providers including advanced practice providers. Use what works for non-healthcare industries like restaurants, amusement parks, and other professional services like hairdresser/barbers for appointment management, template utilization, and cancellation management.

■ Consolidate the many types of insurance managed Medicaid products, to more unified and fewer, to reduce and eliminate unnecessary and confusing variations in approval criteria, conditions covered, billing and coding requirements, and payments for same services provided by same physicians within same specialties.

■ Consider shift *toward* universal health insurance, NOT universal healthcare. Such would allow continued operations of private and academic hospitals (for or non-profit), but standardized insurance coverage (at least basic) with supplemental coverage as needed or desired.

■ Decrease the gap between salaries, wages, and total compensation between those in community-based practices versus hospital-based, particularly those who teach and care for underrepresented minorities, those with lower socioeconomic status, more medical complexities and morbidities, and those in areas that are underserved.

■ Cap hospital CEO and top executive salaries. Make a standardized percentage at risk based on physician and workforce turnover, data indicative of wellbeing, patient safety, and workforce retention instead of based on achieving revenue targets and profit margins (achieved often by elimination of resources and positions, aka "workforce reduction" of physicians, nurses, and frontline workers). Often clinical positions are eliminated first before administrative positions are eliminated. Many hospitals who have a non-profit status enjoy tax-exempt status, yet gap between leader and worker salaries continue to grow, similar to other industries.

■ Support women physicians by providing fully paid FMLA regardless of PTO accrual.

■ Support women physicians who require working part-time and more flexible schedules as needed, while their children are young and/or based on work–life demands and their circumstances.

- Consider flexibility including the ability for physicians to consider working evening clinics and weekends if that allows for increased work–life integration. Hospitals and systems will increase the use of fixed costs and infrastructure. Try to align the workforce across roles so those who prefer working evenings and/or weekends can work together.
- Use report cards and formal feedback from physicians and nurses for their immediate supervisors, administrators, and C-suite executives.
- Simplify billing, coding, and revenue cycle for both government and commercial payers. Incentivize desired outcomes, which is a higher percentage of the population being healthier, and incentivize against readmission, repeated visits, procedures, lab work, ED visits, and excessive or inappropriate use of urgent care and ED. Provide feedback for every acute care visit to urgent care and/or ED to inform whether it was necessary.
- Increase primary and secondary education focused on personal and medical health. Teach students how to self-assess, and take actions against common colds, respiratory illness symptoms, sore throats, body aches, and other general, non-serious, non-critical symptoms.
- Show all employees, expecially physicians, that they are valued, trusted, and respected and that when they need their organization to support them, as they struggle personally and/or professionally, their organization and leaders have their back. Physicians will be loyal, especially when faced with challenges such as the unprecedented pandemic, and show up for their hospitals and systems to ensure patient and public safety, create safe environments to enable safe care, and do their best to achieve what is being asked of them by their employers.
- Ask, listen, and actually respond to concerns. Often in healthcare, physicians and frontline workers are asked to complete annual engagement surveys, yet despite bad scores, and trending of scores in the wrong direction, often the survey asks respondents to comment and share why they are disengaged. Very disheartening and perhaps disrespectful to physicians, is to be asked for their thoughts, feedback, then not acknowledging what they shared nor responding. It's likely more acceptable to physicians if their senior/executive leaders acknowledge their concerns, even explain reasons why actions are not or not yet possible, to address concerns and physician asks, than to never feel acknowledged or have their realities validated.

Conclusion

Despite rapid advances in the treatment of medical and surgical diseases, leveraging technology, artificial intelligence, and "precision medicine" (tailored to an individual's unique genetic makeup) to predict response to medications, the new concept of chronological age versus "medical age", the cost of the US healthcare delivery model continues to rise along with continual worsening of the physician burnout epidemic.

The safety and wellbeing of physicians have not been prioritized, nor systematically addressed across healthcare employers, hospitals, and systems. The current unprecedented public health crisis in the US that deserves prioritization and action, is the rapid attrition of the physician workforce. There are simply not enough doctors to care for the rapidly aging and disproportionately sick US population, in addition to the challenge of disproportionate access to healthcare for several vulnerable subpopulations.

More doctors continue to leave the practice of clinical medicine due to burnout, loss of autonomy, unsustainable workload, pressure, and inability to experience more positive interactions with patients as healthcare delivery has created these sacred encounters as units of "sales" in a culture of productivity-focused business amidst increasing levels of stress and erosion of physician wellbeing on all levels.

To achieve "population health", the US will need not only a seismic *SHIFT* in how we insure and pay for care, as well as how to create more equitable access to quality and affordable care. There must be a focus on reducing waste in how the public utilizes care, and to reduce fraud and stop paying and incentivizing volume but instead reward prevention and achieving actual health. The priority for the society, government, industry, and insurance sector should be an unprecedented focus on the US physician workforce, individually and collectively. Past, current, and future patients, as well as all hospitals and health systems, depend

DOI: 10.4324/9781003452478-17

on a robust and HEALTHY physician workforce as leaders and drivers of the *"performance"* of the US Healthcare System.

Physicians can only achieve highly productive and safe care, with the lowest medical errors, *IF* they themselves experience personal, professional, and psychological safety and optimal wellbeing. Those in service of 350 million Americans deserve and require a unique network of other professionals to help them thrive against the pervasive issues in the culture and business of healthcare. Physicians must be supported, to continue shouldering the immeasurable burden of caring for patients and their sufferings, across physical, mental, emotional, spiritual, cultural, geographical, linguistic, and socioeconomic profiles. Regardless of the types of medical and surgical medicine or practice settings, each of us can take action to support a physician, or many, in our lives and communities.

While by no means are items in each checklist exhaustive, I hope that for physician and non-physician readers, these lists serve as a new perspective and approach which outline actions possible to protect and support a physician. The uniqueness of this approach is to outline and support any physician to create personal, professional, and psychological safety in addition to, or independent of their employers. Even if a hospital and/or system does not "believe" in burnout, or does not provide resources, budgets, or access to professional support specific to the needs of doctors, this book has empowered physicians to live their best lives and increase their career longevity.

By helping physicians protect themselves, I pray and hope all current and future physicians, including those who have walked away from clinical practice due to burnout, can enjoy their careers and not leave the practice of medicine if they wish. Physicians can and should decide their career lengths and "offramp" on their own terms, in the time frame that they wish. A physician will have more flexibility and options to determine when that may be if they have taken action to protect themselves and enjoy financial wellbeing through strategies.

Every physician has touched thousands of lives and already left an individual legacy for countless patients and their families. Thousands of physicians have given discretionary effort in addition to treating patients, to contribute to education, training, ensuring public safety, population health, access to care, advancement of science through research, advocacy, and a multitude of other professional activities that benefit others. They all deserve to live a fulfilled life that isn't simply drowning in tasks and demands not aligned with their core values nor fulfill their hearts with human interactions.

Protecting physicians means we are also protecting their loved ones. For example, effective financial disability and life insurance planning means that even if a physician is diagnosed with terminal cancer, faces mortality despite the best care received, or suffers a tragic premature death, we can live with confidence today that our loved ones will be protected. Most physicians provide all or majority of financial support for their families. There is much solace in knowing that should they suffer career-ending injuries, or acute or chronic health illnesses, both the physician and their family will not have to live in fear of losing their home, being unable to provide for their children and their college education, care for their elderly parents, and/or support their spouses of partners who may have sacrificed their own careers and income by giving up work and professional development to raise a family.

Given that gender inequity persists in pay, career development, academic promotion, career satisfaction, disproportionate child-rearing, and domestic work done, especially for female physicians and surgeons, their already great sacrifices to reach current professional proficiency must be protected as over half of medical school students are female and decades of intentional efforts have finally increased the percentage of women across various surgical and medical subspecialties.

Ensuring physician safety and wellness will impact society in the next decade and beyond. Addressing physician burnout and physician workforce attrition was necessary yesterday, frankly years ago. If we can protect physicians from giving up what they trained for so long to master, to do what they LOVE, to care for as many patients in need as reasonably and in a timely fashion, we will *ALL* be better off. Physician safety, wellbeing, and wellness will serve not only the physicians and their patients but also physician families, colleagues, and countless other healthcare providers across roles, and the communities where physicians live and practice.

A physician's life is a terrible life to waste, or worse, to lose.

Bibliography

Preface

1. https://www.who.int/teams/integrated-health-services/patient-safety/research/safe-surgery
2. Gawande A. (2011). *The Checklist Manifesto*. Profile Books.

Chapter 1

1. Rangel EL, Castillo-Angeles M, Easter SR, et al. Incidence of Infertility and Pregnancy Complications in US Female Surgeons. *JAMA Surg*. 2021;156(10): 905–915. doi:10.1001/jamasurg.2021.3301

Chapter 2

1. Linzer M, Jin JO, Shah P, et al. Trends in Clinician Burnout With Associated Mitigating and Aggravating Factors During the COVID-19 Pandemic. JAMA Health Forum. 2022;3(11):e224163. doi:10.1001/jamahealthforum.2022.4163

Chapter 3

1. Budd J. Burnout Related to Electronic Health Record Use in Primary Care. *J Prim Care Community Health*. 2023 Jan-Dec;14:21501319231166921. doi: 10.1177/21501319231166921. PMID: 37073905; PMCID: PMC10134123.
2. Shanafelt TD, West CP, Dyrbye LN, Trockel M, Tutty M, Wang H, Carlasare LE, Sinsky C. Changes in Burnout and Satisfaction With Work-Life Integration in Physicians During the First 2 Years of the COVID-19 Pandemic. *Mayo Clin Proc*. 2022 Dec;97(12):2248–2258. doi: 10.1016/j.mayocp.2022.09.002. Epub 2022 Sep 14. PMID: 36229269; PMCID: PMC9472795.
3. Sinsky/AMA, https://www.ama-assn.org/practice-management/physician-health/joy-medicine-continuing-reduce-physician-burnout-2023

4. Lirnzer JAMA Health Forum, https://jamanetwork.com/journals/jama-health-forum/fullarticle/2799033
5. Medscape, https://www.medscape.com/slideshow/2022-lifestyle-burnout-6014664
6. Yeleru-gender differences burnout, Yeluru H, Newton HL, Kapoor R. Physician Burnout Through the Female Lens: A Silent Crisis. Front *Public Health.* 2022 May 24;10:880061. doi: 10.3389/fpubh.2022.880061. PMID: 35685758; PMCID:
7. https://www.theatlantic.com/health/archive/2014/09/suicide-and-the-young-physician/380253/
8. Physicians Foundation 2021 survey, https://physiciansfoundation.org/wp-content/uploads/2021/08/2021-Survey-Of-Americas-Physicians-Covid-19-Impact-Edition-A-Year-Later.pdf
9. https://afsp.org/suicide-prevention-for-healthcare-professionals

Additional Resources:

1. https://edhub-ama-assn-org.ezproxy.med.ucf.edu/steps-forward/pages/physician-burnout
2. Advisory Group, https://www.advisory.com/daily-briefing/2022/11/30/clinician-burnout
3. Boston Globe article: 80 hour work week for trainees and impact, https://www.bostonglobe.com/2023/03/26/opinion/rethink-80-hour-workweek-medical-trainees/

Chapter 5

1. https://surgicalergonomics.com
2. https://surgicalcoaching.org/
3. https://doctorsandlitigation.com/
4. https://careersharma.com/
5. https://grangernetwork.com/

Chapter 6

1. Wei JL, Villwock JA. Balance Versus Integration: Work-Life Considerations. *Otolaryngol Clin North Am.* 2021 Aug;54(4):823–837. doi: 10.1016/j.otc.2021.05.007. PMID: 34215359; PMCID: PMC10165858.

Chapter 7

1. Chisholm-Burns MA, Spivey CA, Stallworth S, Zivin JG. Analysis of Educational Debt and Income Among Pharmacists and Other Health Professionals. *Am J Pharm Educ.* 2019 Nov;83(9):7460. doi: 10.5688/ajpe7460. PMID: 31871361; PMCID: PMC6920640.

2. https://www.northstarfinancial.com/advisors/marshall-gifford/
3. https://panaceafinancial.com/resources/how-does-debt-to-income-ratio-affect-doctors

Chapter 11

1. https://www.cdc.gov/niosh/topics/ergonomics/default.html#:~:text=The%20 goal%20of%20ergonomics%20
2. OR Stretches – Between surgery stretches ORStretch.MayoClinic.Com
3. Hallbeck MS, Lowndes BR, Bingener J, Abdelrahman AM, Yu D, Bartley A, Park AE. The Impact of Intraoperative Microbreaks with Exercises on Surgeons: A Multi-center Cohort Study. *Appl Ergon.* 2017 Apr;60:334–341. doi: 10.1016/j. apergo.2016.12.006. Epub 2016 Dec 29. PMID: 28166893.

Additional Citations:

1. Hallbeck MS, Paquet V. Human Factors and Ergonomics in the Operating Room: Contributions that Advance Surgical Practice: Preface. *Appl Ergon.* 2019 Jul;78:248–250. doi: 10.1016/j.apergo.2019.04.007. PMID: 31046956.
2. Hallbeck MS, Law KE, Boughey JC. ASO Author Reflections: Poor Ergonomics During Surgical Procedures May Lead to Work-Related Pain and Early Retirement. *Ann Surg Oncol.* 2020 May;27(5):1327–1328. doi: 10.1245/s10434-020-08277-0. Epub 2020 Feb 28. PMID: 32112208.
3. Schlussel AT, Maykel JA. Ergonomics and Musculoskeletal Health of the Surgeon. *Clin Colon Rectal Surg.* 2019 Nov;32(6):424–434. doi: 10.1055/s-0039-1693026. Epub 2019 Aug 22. PMID: 31686994; PMCID: PMC6824896.

Chapter 12

1. Fletcher L, 2022, *Grace in Grief: Healing and Hope After Miscarriage.* River Grove Books.
2. Rangel EL, Castillo-Angeles M, Easter SR, Atkinson RB, Gosain A, Hu YY, Cooper Z, Dey T, Kim E. Incidence of Infertility and Pregnancy Complications in US Female Surgeons. *JAMA Surg.* 2021 Oct 1;156(10):905–915. doi: 10.1001/ jamasurg.2021.3301. Erratum in: *JAMA Surg.* 2021 Oct 1;156(10):991. PMID: 34319353; PMCID: PMC9382914.
3. Champaloux EP, Acosta AS, Gray ST, Meyer TK, Bergmark RW. Otolaryngology Residents' Experiences of Pregnancy and Return to Work: A Multisite Qualitative Study. *Laryngoscope Investig Otolaryngol.* 2022 Jul 28;7(5):1322–1328. doi: 10.1002/lio2.878. PMID: 36258851; PMCID: PMC9575055.

4. Wei JL, Lavin J, Pearson S, Koehn H, Thompson DM. In Our Own Words – Delaying Pregnancy, Infertility, and Miscarriages. *Int J Pediatr Otorhinolaryngol.* 2023 Dec;175:111769. doi: 10.1016/j.ijporl.2023.111769. Epub 2023 Oct 31. PMID: 37922806.
5. Huh DD, Wang J, Fliotsos MJ, Beal CJ, Boente CS, Wisely CE, De Andrade LM, Lorch AC, Ramanathan S, Reinoso MA, Swamy RN, Waxman EL, Woreta FA, Srikumaran D. Association Between Parental Leave and Ophthalmology Resident Physician Performance. *JAMA Ophthalmol.* 2022 Nov 1;140(11):1066–1075. doi: 10.1001/jamaophthalmol.2022.3778. PMID: 36173610; PMCID: PMC9523550.
6. https://www.ama-assn.org/medical-students/medical-student-health/ama-backs-stronger-leave-policies-medical-students-doctors

Chapter 13

1. https://hbr.org/2005/03/off-ramps-and-on-ramps-keeping-talented-women-on-the-road-to-success

Chapter 14

1. https://news.harvard.edu/gazette/story/2019/07/doctor-burnout-costs-health-care-system-4-6-billion-a-year-harvard-study-says/
2. https://hbr.org/2020/10/what-health-care-can-teach-other-industries-about-preventing-burnout)
3. https://www.theschwartzcenter.org/programs/schwartz-rounds/

Index

Printed in the United States
by Baker & Taylor Publisher Services